Superparenting for ADD

Superparenting for ADD

An Innovative Approach to Raising Your Distracted Child

EDWARD M. HALLOWELL, M.D.
and PETER S. JENSEN, M.D.

BALLANTINE BOOKS · NEW YORK

The information and advice presented in this book are not meant to substitute for the advice of your physician, your child's pediatrician, or other trained health-care professionals. You are advised to consult with health-care professionals with regard to all matters that may require medical attention or diagnosis and to check with a physician before administering or undertaking any course of treatment or making any significant changes in your child's diet.

The names and some identifying characteristics of some of the individuals presented in this book have been changed. Any resulting resemblance to persons living or dead is entirely coincidental and unintentional.

2010 Ballantine Books Trade Paperback Edition
Copyright © 2008 by Edward M. Hallowell, M.D.,
and Peter S. Jensen, M.D.

Published in the United States by Ballantine Books,
an imprint of The Random House Publishing Group,
a division of Random House, Inc., New York.

BALLANTINE and colophon are registered trademarks of
Random House, Inc.

Originally published in hardcover in the United States by
Ballantine Books, an imprint of The Random House
Publishing Group, a division of Random House, Inc., in 2008.

LIBRARY OF CONGRESS CATALOGING-IN-PUBLICATION DATA
Hallowell, Edward M.
Superparenting for ADD : an innovative approach to raising your
distracted child / Edward M. Hallowell and Peter S. Jensen.
        p.   cm.
Includes index.
ISBN 978-0-345-49777-2
1. Attention-deficit hyperactivity disorder—Popular works.
    I. Jensen, Peter S.   II. Title.
RJ506.H9H34484   2008
618.92'8589—dc22   2008035312

Printed in the United States of America on acid-free paper

www.ballantinebooks.com

2 4 6 8 9 7 5 3 1

Book design by Julie Schroeder

For Sue, Lucy, Jack, and Tucker . . .
as always
—Edward Hallowell

Today Matthew is very stubborn. He lies. He never does anything the first five times you ask. He still torments his brother. However, he also holds car washes to raise money for the children in Afghanistan, he wins science fair contests, and he wants to be a policeman, a park ranger, an astronaut, and the president of the United States when he grows up. And you know what? I think he will be.

—A parent of a child who has ADD

Contents

Introduction

Childhood is about unwrapping the gifts you're born with. *Every* child is born with certain gifts, some easy to unwrap, some difficult. Children who have the fascinating trait called ADD (or ADHD, the term that the official diagnostic system used across much of the world) possess extraordinary gifts, but these gifts are unusual in that they can be hidden, and even once found they can be quite difficult to unwrap. In this book, we offer you instructions on how to find and unwrap them.

We do not intend this book to be a comprehensive guide to the treatment of ADD in children. We have both already written our own versions of that. Peter Jensen's include the academically oriented volume entitled *Attention Deficit Hyperactivity Disorder: State of the Science, Best Practices* as well as his comprehensive guide to help parents find the help they need for their children, entitled *Making the System Work for Your Child with ADHD.* Mine include the series I wrote with John Ratey, *Driven to Distraction; Answers to Distraction;* and *Delivered from Distraction,* as well as the book I wrote with Catherine Corman, *Positively ADD.*

We don't want to repeat what's in those books, so we refer you to them for material not presented in this book, such as a detailed discussion of medications, a critical ap-

praisal of alternative and complementary treatments, details
of a proper diagnostic workup, an in-depth discussion of
family problems that typically arise when a child or parent (or both) has ADD, a discussion of the biological and
genetic bases of ADD, speculation on the influence of media
and environment in the causation of ADD and ADD-like
syndromes, advice on the classroom management of ADD, a
discussion of the role of brain scans in diagnosing ADD, an
in-depth discussion of the role of coaching and tutoring, and
various other topics not presented in great depth, if at all,
in this volume.

If all of that isn't in here, what *is* in here? What is in
here is what you need most as a parent (or teacher, or any
concerned person) to bring out the best in your child if your
child has ADD. I've written in my other books about the
need to focus on strengths when dealing with adults who
have ADD. Adults can handle this shift in emphasis, but I
continue to hear from parents of kids with ADD that they
need a more-detailed plan. They want to know what a
strength-based model looks like day in and day out. They
ask me, "What do we *do*?" It is largely in response to that
question that Peter Jensen and I offer this book.

Based on a conviction derived from our combined half
century of experience in working with children who have
ADD, we know that they possess enormous—if often hidden—talents. So this book describes a method by which children who have ADD can do far more than just get by. They
can *thrive*. They can soar beyond where they, their teachers,
and even their parents might have thought they ever could.
By identifying and developing children's interests and inborn abilities, this method draws out the often-camouflaged

talents and strengths of these remarkable children, children who, without the proper kind of help, often languish and lead lives of chronic dissatisfaction, frustration, and under-achievement. But it positively doesn't have to be that way! To the contrary, these kids can achieve at the very highest levels, and lead lives of tremendous success and joy. We emphasize what you need to know to fully unwrap the gifts embedded in those who have ADD. We follow a strength-based approach, which means that we start by looking for talents and only secondarily do we look at what's getting in the way of the development of those talents. This is not commonly emphasized with ADD, and it ought to be. We present a positive, hopeful approach, because our experience as child psychiatrists and as parents of children with ADD, along with Peter's perspective as a scientist studying ADD, has convinced us that this brings far and away the best results.

This book describes an overall approach rooted in the strength-based model, and explains the reasons for endorsing this model as well as a plan for how to use it. Chapter 13 briefly outlines how to make the diagnosis and describes various treatments, but in much less detail than can be found in our other books. The heart of this book is the explanation of a strength-based approach and practical tips on how to use it.

Over the years, parents have given us the most compelling descriptions of what it is like to raise a child who has ADD as well as the most salient advice on how to do it. We have learned more from them, and from their children, than from any other source.

I was, therefore, thrilled when Peter Jensen told me he

had systematically gathered written reports from scores of parents, a few of whom are quoted in this book. As you read what these wonderful parents have to say, you will feel their pain and admire their courage. You will also learn from their advice. You will see how often they know their children possess unacknowledged or undeveloped talents and strengths, and how desperately they seek and need a strength-based model of treatment. You will wince as they speak of their frustration with other people—teachers, doctors, in-laws, grandparents, spouses—who *just don't get it,* and who seem almost intentionally to overlook what a given child might be good at or potentially good at. You will marvel at their tenacity as they recount how many places they had to look before finding the right kind of help. And you will feel hope and joy as you see them and their children score various victories against great odds.

In combining the knowledge and experience of two child psychiatrists, this collaboration brings together authors of different backgrounds. I trained at Harvard and served on the faculty of Harvard Medical School for twenty years, but in my career I have primarily been a clinician who sees patients, as well as an author of some fifteen books. I have ADD and so do two of my children.

Peter is more the scientist and researcher, having served as associate director for child and adolescent research at the National Institute of Mental Health, where he was the lead NIMH investigator on the large Multimodal Treatment of ADHD (MTA) study. In 2000 he became Ruane Professor of Child Psychiatry at Columbia and the director of the Center for the Advancement of Children's Mental Health; in 2007, he was named president and CEO of the REACH Institute

(REsource for Advancing Children's Health). He is the author of more than 250 scientific articles and book chapters and has written or co-edited eighteen books on children's mental health. Two of Peter's children have ADD. Together, we hope our professional and personal experience with ADD will bring a depth of understanding and insight to you in your role as a parent of a child with ADD.

In creating this book, we decided it would be best stylistically for there to be one narrative voice. So while the material presented here emerged from a joint effort, when you hear a first-person narrator, that voice is mine (Edward M. Hallowell's). The term *we* refers to our shared convictions and experiences. Peter Jensen's experiences or recommendations are noted explicitly as such arise. In the few areas where our recommendations or beliefs differ, we make this explicit.

For simplicity's sake, throughout this book we use the term *ADD*, short for *attention deficit disorder*, rather than *ADHD* or *AD/HD*. When we quote other people, they may use the term *ADD* or *ADHD*. The significant point to recognize is that there can be ADD without hyperactivity. In other words, you can have an attention deficit disorder but show no signs whatsoever of hyperactive or impulsive and disruptive behavior. In the diagnostic manual that condition is called *ADHD, inattentive type*—or ADHD without the *H*. To me, that is cumbersome, if not ridiculous. So, unlike Peter, I just use the term *ADD*, and if hyperactivity is part of it in a given individual, I state that it is. Strictly speaking, I ought to call it *ADHD* or *AD/HD*, short for *attention deficit hyperactivity disorder*, because that's the term used in the diagnostic manual. However, since most people in the general public know it as ADD, that's the term we use in this book. When someone we are quoting uses the term *ADHD* or *AD/HD,* don't be confused, as we use the terms interchangeably with *ADD.*

We now welcome you to our collaboration, a collaboration between us authors, you, and the millions of other people who dream of helping every child grow into the best possible person she or he can become. Depending on how it is managed, ADD can be a lifelong curse or it can become a lifelong blessing. We hope that this book helps you and your children turn ADD into a blessing, a gift you completely unwrap.

—Edward M. Hallowell, M.D.
—Peter S. Jensen, M.D.

Superparenting for ADD

Chapter 1

Love

THE ESSENTIAL STRENGTH

Nowhere in life do we see love burn more brightly, work harder, and achieve more than in the relationship between a parent and a child. This is real love. Messy love. Nonstop, never-off-duty love. This love forever changes you. When you have a child, you enter into a permanent state of psychosis. You go crazy. You fall insanely in love with the little baby, whether the baby is adopted or born to you. For first-time parents this love is new and quite unexpected. It's a feeling we've never experienced before. We never knew we could become so selfless, so willing to give up *everything* for our baby. Buoyed by this lifelong, blessed madness, we plunge into the adventure called parenthood. To assist us in doing the most important and most difficult job in the world—raising a child—our single greatest ally is the protean force nature provides parents called love. And what a love it is! We doctors do not celebrate, honor, and emphasize it nearly enough. In this book, however, we do. Here, in our framework, love initiates and supports everything else. Love is the cornerstone of the model we build.

That's because love is the single most powerful tool you can use to draw out your child's strengths. How wonderful that it's free, instantly available, and all but inexhaustible. It doesn't do the whole job, but without it the job never gets done right. Love works unpredictably, in that you have no idea what strengths you are drawing out while you love your child. But if you keep loving and trusting that love, over the years the strengths will emerge. Without love, however, they often do not, or they emerge deformed. So keep your faith in love. Don't ever give up on your child or on the power of love. Sometimes it is all you've got. But no matter how hopeless or desperate you may feel, if you keep on loving, your child's gifts will appear one day, perhaps to your total surprise and the surprise of the world, like wildflowers growing through crevices in a granite rock.

Trust the process love initiates. Always listen for the song your child is trying to sing. Search for the instrument your child is destined to play. Look for the person your child is trying to become.

Those are not just pretty words. They define what matters most in raising children, especially those who have the fascinating, widely misunderstood trait called ADD. These kids particularly need someone who can perceive and draw out what is wonderful within them. It can be a selfless and frustrating process, one that only the best parents and teachers can stick with. But it is also true that *any* parent or teacher can be one of those best parents or teachers.

Some kids slide into life easily. They don't need anyone to listen for the song they are trying to sing because they are born with a song the world already sings, so they naturally join right in. They are born with the instrument they are meant to play. They grow into the wonderful person they are meant to become without a glitch or a crisis. Life is free and easy. They fit in from the start. Good for them!

But then there are those who don't fit in easily, if at all. They bounce back rather than join in. They cause problems for themselves and others. They become the subject of long conversations between various adults, the central theme of which is "What can we do about _____?"

The answer to that question is clear, albeit rarely stated plainly and emphatically: love them. But there's a catch: they're not every minute of every day all that easy to love. Nonetheless, it is love, wise love, smart love, persistent and unremitting love that they need, first and foremost. More than anything else, these kids need someone to detect the beginnings of what's positive in their oddball, offbeat, exasperating, or disruptive ways.

For love to do its transformative work—and *nothing* is more transformative of humankind than love—it must not be blind. It must see clearly and be brave. Through the eyes of this love, you see without illusion the child who stands before you, the child you actually have, as opposed to the child you always wanted or wished you had, and you love *that* child, the messy child, the child who doesn't win the prizes or get the lead role, the child who doesn't get top grades and who isn't necessarily headed for an Ivy League school, the child who can't play the instrument you wanted her to play, who can't throw the fastball you wanted him to throw, nor was ever meant to.

As you come home at the end of the day and your child runs to meet you, it is important before all else that you see not the perfected version of that child or the version you might *like* to behold, but the actual child, the ragtag child who's reaching out to you, the child who needs more than anything to be known and loved for who she or he truly is.

If you give *that* child your love, do you know what a difference you will make? Only all the difference in the world! You will become a miracle maker.

More than anything else, it is love that separates those who thrive in life from those who do not. Love is the main ingredient of the recipe that makes for happy adults. So revel in your love for your child. Enjoy your child. Spend as much time together as you can. Have fun with each other. Work problems out, whatever they might be, knowing that in the long run love will carry the day. This can be difficult, but if you commit yourself to doing it, you will be carrying out the most important and rewarding work in the world. It is work few people will notice, no one will grade you on, and no one will pay you to do. Indeed, your career may suffer if you give loving your child the time it deserves. You may not make CEO or first violin or top billing. But you will be doing the greatest thing a parent can do, which is to give your child the best start in life he or she can get. And on your deathbed, the place where perspective sharpens, you'll rejoice inside that you gave all the love you could to the ones who needed it from you the most—your children.

This is in no way to say that if your child is struggling or if your child gets into major trouble, it's your fault because you haven't loved him enough or loved him right. Not at all. Some children will struggle no matter what. They are born with such problems that no one is able to make them all better. But to give them their best shot, rely on love above all else—love adeptly and creatively applied, love consistently and abidingly offered, love wisely and enthusiastically held out and always felt, even when you're sad, angry, disappointed, or hopeless. Such love is muscular and magical. It stares adversity straight in the eye and never once blinks. It prevails.

As we said above, it is easy to love many kids, but it is not easy to love all of them. Those who have what we call ADD can be dishearteningly difficult to love at times, but these are the kids who need your love the most, because they get it elsewhere the least.

Even though love is the best "treatment" we've got for just about anything, there are several reasons that love doesn't get more mention from doctors and other experts as a treatment for ADD (or any other condition, for that matter). First, it's hard to define what love is, and it is therefore difficult to prescribe. Second, it is difficult to measure the results of applying it. And third, perhaps most important, love is not a quick fix. Most treatments that get studied scientifically in a prospective, double-blind, randomized trial produce results fairly rapidly, even within hours in the case of some medications, or within months or at most a year or two. Love doesn't. Love is slow. Love often seems to be getting nowhere. It can take decades before you see the payoff for all those years of loving. The scientific study would have deemed your efforts useless long before you got to see the positive results.

And so experts recommend various complicated fix-it plans, rife with charts, scripts, and the latest new thing, which parents read and study and try to implement, all the while with a sinking feeling in their gut because they know this latest plan won't do much. They do their best to put it into action, because they need to try *something,* and yet they know it's missing an essential element.

That essential element is the total child. Many of our scientifically established treatments are so directed at fixing shortcomings that the talents, charms, and core self of the child get ignored. What's missing is the positive essence of the child. These treatment plans are ineffective—and grim—because they are not fueled with the positive vision of what a great kid is in the making. It's disheartening to set up all these complicated interventions and carry out all these laborious treatment plans because they so miss the point of childhood: a time to explore and dream, a time to get into and out of mischief and funny places, a time when everything is possible and impossible all at once, a time to be king or queen of all the fields and skies and seas, a time when what matters so very much to grown-ups really doesn't matter so very much at all. If you had that time once in your life, that time called childhood, your capacity to dream and feast upon very little never dies.

Rather than setting out to preserve and protect childhood, rather than setting out to develop and celebrate the child's unique and individual strengths, these well-meaning treatment plans often drive along on square adult wheels, pedantically trying to turn lists, reminders, incentives, consequences, and the achievement of quarterly numbers into the stuff a child can grow on.

These plans are driven not by a vision of bringing out the best in each child but by a fear that a child will fail in life if he doesn't learn to shape up and do things right, now and on schedule. So all efforts turn toward standardization, normalization, testing, and assessing. The more a child falls behind, the more he gets "help" to do better, which means to become more like the kids who aren't falling behind. No one stops to think that maybe what works for the other kids just doesn't work for this kid. No one stops to think that maybe the kid who is falling behind has talents that could come out if he were dealt with in a different way.

It is time for that to change. It is time for us to acknowledge that *every* child has gifts. It is time for us, the adults who care for children, to make it our business to discover and unwrap those gifts, no matter how difficult or frustrating doing that might be. It is time for us to develop child-rearing practices and school curricula that bring out the best in every child, knowing that every child has a best. This is a noble goal, a reachable goal, and one far superior to the mediocre, joyless, conformist, fear-driven goals of many educational and child-rearing plans in the United States today.

I went to high school with a kid who got mostly Cs and Ds and sometimes Fs. It took him five years to complete the four-year curriculum. He couldn't do math, he couldn't do foreign languages, he couldn't spell. Socially, he compensated by making jokes about how stupid he was. Finally he graduated by the skin of his teeth.

His name is John Irving. He is now acclaimed as one of the world's great novelists. But when he graduated from high school, he thought he was stupid. Others might have judged him a loser, a young man on his way to nowhere.

Instead, he unwrapped his considerable gifts. How? You'd have to ask him to be sure, but from all that I have learned about his life, it was because of love. His two parents never lost faith in him. They *always* believed in him.

And rather than fussing too much over his poor grades and other shortcomings, they put their energy into supporting his strengths, one of which was wrestling. I can still see his mother sitting in the front row at wrestling meets, cheering like a rabid fan not only for John but also for all the other members of the team, match after match.

And the wrestling coach, a legend in New England wrestling by the name of Ted Seabrooke, took John under his wing and gave him a place where he could achieve mastery, and the confidence and optimism that that engenders. Irving is now himself legendary not only for his imaginative powers but also for his work ethic as a writer. I wonder how much of that came from those years with Seabrooke. As a teen with an undiagnosed learning disability, John discovered that hard work does pay off, especially if you apply it in an area of your strengths, which wrestling was at that time for him.

The combination of identifying strengths, creating a chance to succeed, and fueling the process with optimism and excitement leads to success and happiness most of the time. But it starts with love. Just think of John's mom sitting there matside, match after match after match, giving her son who was struggling academically a chance to feel joy and pride in what he could do well.

You can depend upon it: nothing works better than love. Our most common advice to parents who are having ongoing trouble with a difficult child is "Hang in there. Keep loving him. Keep showing up. Keep trying. Keep setting limits, offering new ideas, making deals, wrestling with one catastrophe after another. Just don't give up. Don't write him off. One day all your love and all your efforts—and his—will pay off." Sometimes these parents get annoyed with us for giving this advice. They already know that, they say, and they want something more esoteric, something more elaborate, something new that will work. And I do have various new interventions to offer. But none of them is worth a nickel without love.

I've been in this business long enough—I started treating patients in 1978—to know that I'm right. I've seen teens go to jail but, because one parent hung in there and kept loving them, find great careers for themselves years later. I've seen children with ADD get tossed out of school after school, their parents told each time that this child is the "worst" (the actual word used) the school has ever seen, only at age twenty-five to own a million-dollar business and be as happy as can be. I've seen adolescents with ADD get so depressed that they wanted to commit suicide and even try it, only years later to be helping me counsel other adolescents on how much better life can get. I've seen girls curl up on the floor of my office crying, pounding their heads, saying how stupid they are and how life sucks and how they wish they were dead, only years later to be sitting in a chair in that same office telling me about their medical school acceptance, their upcoming marriage, or their having started their own business. I've seen boys spend most of their teens smoking pot and doing very little else, only in their twenties to find the right job and the right girl and turn life into a spectacular success.

The difference—*every time*—is love, love applied by someone, somewhere, somehow. Sure, treatments help, and help a lot. As the child psychiatrist and researcher, Peter Jensen tends to recommend scientifically proven treatments, such as carefully monitored medication and various forms of behavior therapy—using rewards and consequences to teach the child better behavioral control. I recommend whatever works, as long as it is safe and legal. I offer medication, I offer neurofeedback, I offer cerebellar stimulation, I offer nutritional supplements, I offer behavioral therapy, group therapy, couples counseling, family therapy, individual therapy; I offer coaching and tutoring, I suggest martial arts training, and I am always on the lookout for new and potentially useful interventions to help people who have ADD. But above all else we recommend love, because love makes the biggest difference. People who get love usually do well sooner or later. People who don't get love too often don't.

"Love your child for who he or she is, and try hard to keep that in mind when the times get rough. You, sometimes, are all they have. Their behavior is usually not willful, and they are not able to see themselves as their world does. How frustrating it must be to not truly understand why everyone is mad at you and to feel like you haven't been let in on the secret. Get in a support group. It is helpful for you and your child to know that you're not the only ones who live like this. Never, never give up! There are some valuable lifelong lessons to learn. Put your experiences and successes to good use!"

—Sally, mother of a son with ADD

But since it's hard to define and hard to prescribe, how do we suggest that you learn to give love in the right way?

Try to catch on to the spirit and essence of your child. Spend time with your child just being there. Watch, listen, and interact, but don't direct or worry about getting things done. Just hang out with each other. You'll soon feel who your child is. Parents, more than anyone else, can sense who their child truly is. Before he gets labeled smart or stupid, hardworking or lazy, athletic or a klutz, friendly or taciturn, engaging or standoffish, before he gets labeled ADD or XYZ, a parent usually senses the beginnings of who this child really is and what she is all about. Hold on to that! Don't listen too closely to the labelers and diagnosticians. We know about them; we are two of them. Out of necessity, we oversimplify; therefore in our diagnoses we miss the subtleties, the complexities, the richness that goes into what we call the spirit and essence of a child. If you don't attend to the spirit and essence, they can get trampled on and quite easily destroyed. It is tragic how many children lose their spirit and essence growing up. You can protect that mainly by noticing it, naming it, and nourishing it. Doing that is what we mean by love.

It can sound like this:

"Sarah, you are so kind. When I was tearing up at Gammy's funeral and you handed me that Kleenex, that was just so nice."

"Tommy, you have a real knack with puzzles. I don't know how you put that one together so fast."

"Holly, you see colors better than anyone I know. All I saw was green, but you saw a hundred shades of green."

"Tucker, you never give up. It's amazing how you just keep at it, whatever it is."

"Lucy, you notice everything. Nothing escapes your eye."

"Jack, you are a master builder. What you did with that sand castle is just amazing."

Simply noticing early and often whatever special talents and interests your child may show actually makes those qualities take root and grow. On the other hand, sad to say, if those qualities do not gain notice, they may not take root, and they may die. Noticing is to the growth of talent what sunshine is to the growth of a plant.

It is often forgotten that one of the most useful ways a parent can love a child is merely to notice who she is or what he does. It's easy—but it is seldom given the top billing it deserves. Parents can get so preoccupied with what they want their children to do or who they want them to become that they overlook what they're already doing that's potentially worthwhile and who they actually are.

> "The best advice we got was that if we ever needed help, we should ask for it, because there was always something we could figure out together that could help. The worst thing would be to allow ourselves to become so frustrated with our son's behavior that we would stop loving him."
>
> —Marlene, mother of a son with ADD

As a parent, you probably have no idea how powerful your noticing, smiling presence can be. If your child has ADD (or anything else, for that matter), use your sympathetic imagination to try to see the beginnings of a flourishing adult in the scuffling and shuffling of the child you now have. Visualize your child grown up, not as the goof-off or criminal you fear he or she might become but as the best adult you can imagine him or her turning into. Imagine in what ways this child, this disorganized, stubborn, unheeding, inappropriate, misspeaking, and misdoing galumph, already has the makings of a superb you-name-it.

It is not you who will name it. It is your child, given the chance. However, it is you—is it ever you!—who can provide that chance, who can make it possible for that galumph to become the superb whatever-it-is that that galumph is trying to become. If you don't ride shotgun for your child, if you let the world and its enforcers have their way with him or her, your child *might* still turn into a superb adult, because kids with ADD don't give up easily, but, on the other hand, he or she just might not. The world can disassemble the spirit of a child, even a tenacious and valiant child. It can force children to knuckle under, thereby sacrificing the one and only chance they have to become the person they were meant to be. Few things are as sad as the sight of adults leading a masquerade life, a life of trying to be someone they were never meant to be, of trying to keep up and be "normal" when they were meant to be so much more than that.

A personal experience of Peter Jensen's showcases how important it is to love your child in a way that speaks to him or her. It also showcases the fact that it often takes trial and error to find the right way to communicate your love, and then years—a seeming lifetime—to know that your love has made a difference in your child's life.

Peter's son David has ADD. He and his father often clashed when David was young. As even David now acknowledges, he was often mean to his siblings—he provoked them and was physically aggressive toward them. Even so, Peter himself can now acknowledge that he was too quick to blame David, to assume that he was always the perpetrator responsible for his siblings' injuries or tears. On more than one unhappy occasion, Peter lost his temper, shouting, spanking, and scaring his son into submission and better behavior. Disturbed by his *own* reaction to David's behavior, Peter sought therapy to control his temper, and did his best to apologize to his son—and his other kids—for behavior he hoped they wouldn't emulate. In addition, he tried to institute new rules—star charts, rewards, clear consequences— around the house. With David, however, the die was cast, at least temporarily. Good behavior came as a result of being scared of and scared away from a close relationship with his father.

With the benefit of many years' perspective, Peter and David can both see that Peter's too-often short temper with his son made David feel misunderstood at best, unloved at worst. With uncanny insight, a very young David—eight years old at the time—put it best when he told his father: "Dad, sometimes when you consequence me or take points away, it just makes me want to be badder."

As Peter puts it, "My behavior therapies were backfiring because they weren't working within *his* model. They created a sense, in his mind, of unfairness and of being artificially manipulated. I just knew that somehow, as much as I loved him, I didn't love him in such a way that he felt truly loved."

When David was fourteen, he and his younger brother Jonathan were Boy Scouts and Peter signed on to be their scoutmaster. In order to not appear to play favorites with his kids, Peter called his sons "Mr. Jensen," just as he used

Mr. before the last names of all the other Scouts. It was awkward and contrived, but it was Peter's careful attempt to create a level playing field within the troop.

"But," Peter now relates, "it also triggered something in David, something that is easily triggered in kids with ADD. He didn't like the forced and false formality, and he didn't like my attempts to manipulate the situation—just as he had not warmed to the star charts and rewards systems. David was beginning to assert his own needs again, increasingly saying, 'This is stupid, this Scout stuff.' One day as we were organizing our activities, David grabbed a basketball and said, 'Hey, guys, don't do that stupid knot-tying stuff. Let's go play basketball. Come on over here with me.' So now I have my own son becoming the active ringleader of a revolt in front of everyone! I was extremely angry and felt my old temper rising to the surface. I was totally struggling within myself. I knew I needed to deal with David without going down those old paths.

"That night, I asked David to come up to my room. I decided I had to talk with him in a different way than he and I had done years before. So I knew that I couldn't get angry, and I didn't. I just told him my dilemma. As I was holding back tears, I said, 'You know, David, I wanted to do this Scout thing because I wanted to have special time with you and Jon. And it's just not working. It's not working the way I hoped it would. You're my most challenging Scout.'"

David is now, at this writing, thirty, married, and a father himself. Recently, he told Peter (on Father's Day) that he remembered well that teary discussion. Although Peter couldn't be sure of it at the time, David assured him that it was at that moment that he *knew* his father loved him.

"When you called me up to your room," he said, "I figured you were going to chew me out, but you didn't. You got through to my heart."

"That story isn't scientific evidence," Peter says, "but it underpins my unshakable conviction that there's crucial stuff we just don't know how to measure. The little, subtle shifts that I made in my behavior, the shifts an observer couldn't and wouldn't see, become like the turning of an ocean liner. You don't see the changes when the wheel is turned a few degrees. You don't see the dramatic difference in the *Queen Mary*'s course, but you end up in Lisbon instead of London.

"Clinicians and parents shouldn't think so much about shaping and changing behavior but should instead think about shaping and changing a relationship." I so agree. Parents go to see doctors in the hope of getting their children to obey them, to do what's right, to improve their scores or their performance. A common question we are asked by parents is, "How can I get my child to do what he's supposed to do?" Of course, we do have various answers to that question. But underpinning every such intervention must be an emotion, a feeling. It is the feeling of positive connection, a feeling of being cared for no matter what, a preverbal sense of belonging to something positive that's larger than yourself. If a child—or a person of any age, for that matter—has that feeling, right action will eventually follow. Too often, parents skip over the feeling and focus totally on trying to control the behavior.

"The whole idea," Peter summarized, "is that you have to capture the heart before you can open the head for change. And that's what my son was saying when he told me, 'Dad, when you behavior-therapy me, it makes me want to be badder.' I hadn't captured his heart. We have to use a model that says you have to love these children first. That doesn't mean bribing or spoiling. It doesn't mean giving in or not setting limits or being permissive. It simply means acting out of love."

A parent ought to be a child's first and greatest fan. A man was once asked how he had achieved so much in his life. He replied, "In my mother's eyes, I only saw smiles." That's where a great life begins: in loving eyes.

Chapter 2

Loving Your Child in the Face of Opposition

I have ADD. My daughter and one of my sons have ADD. In my daily practice, I see and treat kids with ADD. Just being with them usually makes me smile. They invariably have a special something, a spark, a delightful quirk—which they sometimes try to hide, but which I usually can find. Then they relax, brighten up, and make me laugh and learn. Indeed, I think that people with ADD represent some of the most fascinating, fun, and fulfilling of all the people I meet.

If you have a child with ADD, it's important that you help that child feel good about who he or she is and what to expect in life. It's important that you search out and promote the positives—both about life and about your child—even as you deal with the all-too-obvious negatives. If your child feels good about who he is and about what life has to offer, he will do far better than if he does not.

My son Jack has ADD. I'll never forget when his seventh-grade English teacher asked all the students in his class to write down adjectives describing themselves. When they were done, she asked them to circle the three qualities they were most proud of. Jack circled *creative, athletic,* and *ADD*. Bingo! I knew he was on the right path.

But as much as we love children who have ADD, we also know how difficult, at times impossibly difficult, it can be to raise them. Just as we know how charming and creative they can be, we also know what a trial they can be. We know how exhausting life can be when you have just one child who has ADD, let alone more than that, or if your spouse has it, too. And it is often the case that your spouse will have it, because ADD is highly heritable, so often one or both parents supplied the genes.

What's hard in raising a child who has ADD? If you have a child with ADD, we probably don't have to tell you. Small and large issues give us trouble. Small issues that we can't seem to resolve get bigger; big issues are often divisive and destructive. No doubt you'll recognize your own experience here:

The answer to the question "How many times do I have to tell you?" is: about two thousand.

Socks migrate. You will find odd socks in the attic, in the basement, behind the washer, in the freezer, in the toilet tank, under a rock outside, in the car, or just about anywhere except neatly rolled up in the drawer reserved for them.

Teachers don't understand. Good teachers. Master teachers. After you have spent an hour explaining ADD to them, or after they have listened, understood, and appreciated a lecture on ADD from a guest expert, they will send home a note about your son the *very next day* that reads,

"Will needs to pay better attention in class. He needs to focus his mind better. Unless he tries harder, he will not achieve success. He is letting himself, you, and the school down. I would like to see his attitude improve in this regard. Please urge him to pay attention." It can seem that what I call the "moral model"—that your child's ADD is somehow something he or she is not *willing* to overcome, and/or that it is a result of something that you as a parent are not doing right—is burned into the brain of many teachers and that understanding ADD as a biological difference in wiring goes against one of the ten commandments of teaching.

Forget about teachers, because even *you* don't understand. You can't really fathom why your son or daughter behaves in such an inconsistent, self-sabotaging way. How can he or she be perfectly prepared for the test the night before, only to forget *everything* while taking the test? How is that possible? Must there not be some terrible force at work, some force of self-destruction? How can anyone waste his or her talents so foolishly? Why doesn't your child buckle down and try harder and get his or her act together and stop being so exasperating and frustrating? Then you listen to a lecture or read a book, and you say, "Oh, I see, now I get it." And then, of course, even *you* forget it. Just like your son or daughter forgets what's on the test—only you don't have ADD.

Your mother doesn't understand. Boy, does she ever not understand. "All he needs is discipline. You remember what I would do if you ever did that?" You remember. You shudder. You're glad your mom is not in charge anymore.

"One of the hardest things about accepting my child's ADD is that there is no concrete test for it. Because of this, many people do not believe that it is a real disease. When I tell people (including my mother-in-law) that my son has ADD, they will roll their eyes and say that all children are active and that I just have to control him better. There is no other disease that I can think of that people look down on you when you give your child medicine to help him. The media don't help, either!"

—Sarah, mother of a son with ADD

Your spouse doesn't understand. Let's say you are the wife and you know your husband has ADD (it is often the other way around; many women have ADD). But, of course, he doesn't *believe in* ADD—as though it were something like a religious principle, a matter of belief. Still, that's what he says as he eats his dinner and mutters about what *his* father would have done if *he* ever brought home grades like that. And you're glad neither he nor his father is in charge. But you don't want to have to be so much in charge yourself, and you keep trying to figure out ways to get your husband to see the light and get help with his ADD.

Homework expands. In your son's hands, homework is like some strange substance that grows the more you try to cut it down to size. Your son works on his homework for three hours and then shows you what he's done, which is almost nothing that was supposed to be done.

When you scream, "Why didn't you spend those three hours doing the homework that was supposed to be done?" he looks at you and gives you the most honest answer in the world of ADD to all "why" questions: "I don't know." That's the truth. He *doesn't* know. Which only makes you feel like going more ballistic.

Time is different. In the world of ADD there are really only two times: *now* and *not now.* Test in a week? *Not now.* While a child who doesn't have ADD will start to plan how to get ready for the test, the child who has ADD waits until the test enters the zone of *now* and then, in a panic, starts to prepare. Actually, this sometimes works, because in a panic you pump out a lot of adrenaline, which is nature's own stimulant medication, a lot like Ritalin or Adderall.

Words such as *structure, supervision, reminders,* and *persistence* don't even begin to describe the magnitude of the task you have to tackle every day. While *all* children need structure and supervision, and while *all* children need reminders from parents who are persistent, children who have ADD need extra structure, megasupervision, constant reminders, and parents who exhibit the persistence that only a parent's love can produce. Your job is so much greater than you ever expected, so much more taxing than anyone ever explained, that it is hard on some days not to want to give up.

Of course you don't give up. But why? Because it isn't in you to do that. Life would be so much easier if it were . . . but this is your child we're talking about, and you just can't give up on him or her.

You ask, "How long will it take?" You ask this, what, every day? "How long before he _____?" It makes me think of the Supremes song "You Can't Hurry Love." It's especially true of this kind of love, the extraordinary kind of love parents give. You have to hang in there with your child, loving in the face of all kinds of adversity, even mean comments from people you like and admire.

People say stupid things. It is very hard to listen to some of the comments people make about your child who has ADD. You have to be careful in how you respond, because you are trying to build bridges, not burn them. Still, it is tempting to do a little burning now and then.

Vacations can be hell. You just have to get used to the fact that sometimes your child is going to turn a hotel room into a disaster zone, a restaurant into a bowling alley, and an airplane into an airplane you wish would crash.

"What's best" has almost no meaning, as in "Why don't you do what's best for you?" The ruling principle in the world of ADD is what's engaging, not what's best. Teaching what's best is hard.

You lose your sense of humor. Oh, boy, when that happens you are in *deep* trouble. You've got to be able to laugh to raise a child who has ADD. Sometimes your sense of humor is all that stands between you and going nuts.

What else is hard? Reading all the books you're supposed to read is hard. So much information. So much advice. So little help!

Most of all, you worry. All parents worry, but you take worry to a whole new level. You read about how many kids with ADD go to jail, get into car accidents, get hooked on drugs, never graduate from college or never even go, get fired from multiple jobs, can't stay in relationships, get depressed, attempt suicide, or just generally lead lousy lives, and you worry, *What can I do to prevent that?* and then you worry that the true and honest answer to that question is *Not much.* You hope and pray that the medication you don't even want to give your son can somehow prevent all these bad outcomes, and then you worry that he isn't taking it anyway, and you worry that there's really nothing you can do except try to get the meds into him and hope they don't turn out to cause brain damage or cancer. Then along comes someone like me who claims that ADD can be a *gift* and that all your love is the starting point in unwrapping the gift, and you hope and pray that I'm not a charlatan who's full of hot air. I tell you that I'm not. I tell you that I've been around the block on this maybe more than anyone else you'll ever find. You start to believe me, but then you worry that if I were full of hot air, well, I wouldn't *tell* you, would I? Maybe I wouldn't even know it. So where does that leave you? It leaves you with worry. And that worry can become toxic.

You need someone like one of us to tell you something more useful than that you worry, so we will. Let us start by giving you four simple steps to control toxic worry. You don't want to eliminate worry completely; we call that denial. Some worry is good because it alerts you to problems and leads you to prevent or solve them. But worry can become toxic. If it does, we recommend the following four steps:

1. Talk to someone. Never worry alone. Worry gets *extremely* toxic when you worry alone.
2. Get the facts. Toxic worry is usually based on wrong information or lack of information.
3. Make a plan. If you have a plan, you automatically feel more in control and less worried. It doesn't matter if the plan fails. You just make a new plan. Life is all about revising plans. Just always have a plan to deal

with the problem. Stay out of the passive position.
Toxic worry feasts on people in passive mode.

4. Surround yourself with people who can laugh. It
   is important to be able to regain a perspective that
   allows you to see the humor in all of the messes
   these kids can get into.

Raising kids who have ADD is a marathon, not a sprint.
At the same time, if you use the principles advanced in this
book, the chances are excellent that you and your child will
not only survive but also thrive.

I can say that with confidence because I have been down
this road many times with many parents and many children,
thousands of them over my twenty-five years of practice.
Both Peter and I know how hard it can be, but we also know
that if you keep on loving, if you never give up, if you never
worry alone, and if you learn from your mistakes, not only
can you and your child make it, you can also win.

Chapter 3

Developing Empathy

WHAT IT'S LIKE TO BE A KID WITH ADD

The starting point in demonstrating your love and in developing a strength-based approach is empathy. As a parent—or teacher, or anyone else—if you want a kid to open up to you, you need to have a feel for what it's like to be that kid. In the case of ADD this is particularly crucial, because these kids get a steady diet of judgments and recommendations based on *no understanding whatsoever* of what it's like to be who they are.

Before making recommendations, no matter how constructive and well-meaning they may be, it is imperative first of all to establish some rapport, and the best way to do that is by letting the other person know that you have an idea, some inkling at least, of what it's like to spend a day in his or her shoes.

Because most adults who do not have ADD haven't a clue as to what it's like to have ADD, I offer this fictional soliloquy from a high school student who has ADD. A composite, it is rooted in true-to-life experience, both our own and that of the thousands of kids we've met who have ADD.

It should give you a pretty good idea of what it's like to have this beguiling condition.

"What's it like to have ADD? See, I don't really know what ADD is. So I'll just tell you what it's like to be me. Life's a gas. My mom worries that I'm depressed and my self-esteem and stuff like that is bad, but I actually love my life. I just hate school. And some people. Well, I don't hate them, I just have *trouble* with people who don't get it, you know, people who don't get the basic deal, people who can't see the other side of a donut without turning it around. It's amazing how clear things can be to me, but they're just not to some people. I don't know. It's not a matter of me thinking I'm *right,* it's just a matter of me seeing as obvious stuff that other people don't see at all. It's weird, because then I get in trouble sometimes for saying what I see.

"School has always sucked for me. Is it cool with you to say *sucked*? I don't mean to offend you, you know. I don't mean to offend anyone. I get told I offend people all the time, but I *really* don't mean to. Why would I mean to? It doesn't help me any to make people mad at me. But what I can't believe is how incredibly uptight and stupid some people are. But I don't even want to offend *them.* I just want to get along. You know, who doesn't?

"The thing is, what's hard for most people is easy for me and what's easy for most people is, like, *really hard* for me. Take something that's supposedly easy, like remembering what day it is. That's easy, right? Well, it isn't always easy for me! I'll think it's, like, Tuesday, when actually it's Thursday. I mean, Tuesday and Thursday just don't have separate places in my brain like they do for most people. They both begin with *T* and neither one is on the weekend, so what's the difference? Even the calendar gets confused and has to call them *TU* and *TH,* when the other weekdays you can tell with just one letter, you know, *M* or *W* or *F.* So if even the calendar takes extra time with Tuesday and Thursday, so what if I can't always tell the difference? But if I tell most people that, they look at me like I'm *completely* crazy or just a total retard or like I'm trying to be a wise guy and make trouble. But you tell me, what exactly is the difference between Tuesday and Thursday? There's no real difference. They're days in the week, and that's cool, it's good to have days in the week, whoever thought of having days in the week was a genius, man, but once we have the days in the week, does it really matter, you know, *which* day in the week it is? Sure, you have to know where to go when, and so I guess in that way it matters which day it is, but some people just get so hung up on which day it is, like that's the most important thing in their lives, and they start every day memorizing which day it is and that's what they think about on the ride to school or to work or wherever they're going, they sit there thinking and memorizing which day it is, and when someone comes along like me who doesn't necessarily know which day it actually is all the time, they look at me like I'm so *weird,* like I'm an alien or some kind of a threat, like a *dangerous person,* and I can tell they think I ought to go live on a junk heap because I don't necessarily know which *day* it is, when they've spent all morning making sure they know.

"Or, you know, other things, like did I leave a kitchen cabinet open, that's one my mother thinks I really ought to be able to know unless I'm just being a jerk, but honest to God I can take a jar of peanut butter and a loaf of bread out of the cupboard, make toast, spread it with peanut butter, reach up into another cupboard and get a plate, because Mom has this *thing* about wanting me to put food on a plate, and then I can open another cupboard and get a glass because, like the plate thing, Mom has a thing about not wanting me to drink milk out of the carton so I put it into a nice tall glass, and then I take my snack and go down to the basement to turn on the TV, and like I said, I don't even *think* about whether or not the cupboard doors are open. It's not like I see them open and say to myself, *Screw that, who cares about those doors, they're just dumb doors.* I *want* to close them because I know Mom has a thing about that and I don't want to get her mad at me, but I just don't think about those doors, I just leave the kitchen and head downstairs with my mind on other things.

"Same thing with faucets. Same thing with lights. Same thing with dirty laundry, you know, socks, underwear, towels. I honestly don't know where I put those things. I take them off, you know, and of course they go somewhere, but it doesn't feel like I *put* them somewhere. You know, if you say you put something somewhere it sounds like you decided to do it, to put it wherever you put it, but I take my clothes off me and that's pretty much where my thinking ends. Does this make me sick? I don't know. I don't feel sick. To tell you the truth, I kind of feel bad for the people who really get *into* where they're going to put their laundry and they have, like, this whole *plan* in their minds, you know, socks here, boxers there, towels on this shelf, shirts here . . . ooooh, man, *that* sounds kind of off to me. I mean, when you think about it, what have they got going on inside their heads? Kitchen cabinet door, closed. Faucet, off. Light switch, check. Socks, ditto. If you ask me, that's freaky.

"I don't know how they do it, but whatever they do, it sure pays off in school. 'Cause that's what school, like, *really admires*. Be on time. Hand in the right paper to the right person on the right day. It almost doesn't matter what you write in your papers—if you can do that other stuff, you'll never be in trouble. It's all about whether you can remember every little detail, even though it has no relevance to anything you care about. All you're supposed to care about is that it matters to the people who want you to care about it, and since they hold your future in their hands, you are supposed to care about whatever they want you to care about, and the more ridiculous it is, if you can still care about it, the better grade you'll get. It's even better if you can pretend that *you* really care about it, too. Like if you can say, 'Monsieur Thomas, I really like memorizing the genders of these French nouns, because we don't have to do that in English and it makes me a better person to know the genders of French nouns,' like you think it's really cool, even though you know inside it is *the* most boring thing you could possibly do. Then when I raise my hand after that kid has kissed up and I say, 'Monsieur Thomas, I have to say I don't get the same thrill Marc over there gets out of this gender thing. Is there any way I could skip it and Marc could do mine, too?' I get into trouble and Marc gets a great rec for his college application.

"Then my mom tells me how stupid I was to say that, and I say it was just what everyone else was thinking, and she says, 'I know, but why did *you* have to be the one to say it?' and the honest answer to that is, *I don't know. But I did have to say it.* That's another thing that's different about me, and maybe it's ADD, I guess. I just *have* to say some things. It's not like I plan it. Geez, if I *planned* it, I wouldn't say it at all. Like with Monsieur Thomas, if I had thought about it, I would have known that he wasn't going to appreciate what I had to say. But I didn't think about it, I just said it. This is what my mom doesn't understand. She says, 'Don't you see how this just gives you a bad reputation and gives people who don't like you justification for the bad things they say about you?' and she's right, I know that, and I love her for trying to save me from myself, but that's who I am. I say what's on my mind and what I see. Sometimes I feel bad about that 'cause it gets me into trouble and I guess it will keep me out of some colleges, but, you know what, I'm kind of proud of who I am. Is it so bad to be honest? Whatever, I can't change it, that's for sure.

"That's the part most people don't understand. Even teachers who *like* me, like Mr. Jenkins, my chemistry teacher, he'll tell me just to get more discipline, but I tell him, 'Mr. Jenkins, I'm *trying,*' and he'll stop and say he's sorry for saying that, because he knows I am, and then he'll try to teach me tricks and stuff to help me with what's hard for me.

"But then, what's easy for me is hard for other kids. Like do you ever watch *The Simpsons* or *South Park*? I could write for those shows. Most people, even if they happen to like those shows, would have no idea how to come up with the lines. Whoever came up with Eric Cartman, that guy's a genius, but, you know, I could see myself doing that, too. I don't mean to sound conceited. How could *I* sound conceited, right? I know I'm not a genius, no way. Believe me, if school has taught me one thing, it's that I am not a genius. They might as well have made me write a hundred times on the blackboard, 'I am not a genius.' But I know I could come up with characters for shows like *South Park* and stuff, and I know that most other random people couldn't. Hey, they probably wouldn't *want* to. They'd think it means you're sick or weird. But it really doesn't. It's just the way my mind works. I think of different stuff.

"Like when the teacher is talking, let's say she's talking about, you know, the causes of the Civil War. Now, that war is pretty interesting when you think about it, how a whole *country* could get into, like, a family feud, and, you know, was it about slaves or was it really about money, and how did that Lincoln dude pull it all together, that's pretty interesting, I'm not saying it isn't because I think it is and I've even read books about it, but when Ms. Binkley starts to lecture to us about it, I just *can't* listen to her. I'll watch her lips move, and I'll start looking really closely at her teeth 'cause she has this one tooth that really sticks way out, she really ought to see a dentist, man, 'cause she'd look a lot better if she just got that fixed, and then I start wondering why she doesn't get it fixed, is it that she can't afford it? That's pretty sad, or maybe she's so clueless she's not, like, *aware* of how strange it looks, like some kind of half-vampire look, or maybe she's married to some weird dude who gets off on a tooth that sticks out, but that couldn't really be true, could it, so then I start to feel bad for her, like she's probably alone in her life because of this tooth, and how if she just got it fixed her life could, like, *really change,* and it's sad she's alone because of a tooth, but maybe she's proud of it, maybe having that tooth stick out is her way of saying, 'Love me, love my tooth,' and that's like her test of people, and I wonder who will be the guy who passes that test, could be like a blind person, but then that wouldn't count as passing the test 'cause he wouldn't know how ugly what he was getting was, visually that is, so she would probably want someone who could, you know, *see* the tooth and love her anyway, and I'll be thinking about this, when, *bingo*, she calls on me. Of course, I have no idea what she's asked me or what's been going on 'cause I've been thinking about how to get her hooked up, but even I am with it enough not to say *that*, so I just say, 'Please repeat the question,' and she makes a little clicking sound with her tongue, like, *There he goes again, daydreaming and not being a serious student,* and she calls on someone else. That's my life in school."

Chapter 4

The Right Kind of Help

While the essential elements in a positive parent-child relationship are love and empathy, a loving parent will also seek expert advice if a child struggles in some way. In the case of a child who might have ADD, this is a crucial juncture; you must get reliable advice, and you need to be able to trust and feel good about the professional who evaluates your child. Now is the time when a strength-based model of assessing and understanding your child's mind becomes life-changing. A deficit-based model can lead to years of joyless "treatments," while a strength-based model opens the way for joyful, if difficult, years of the unwrapping of gifts.

The kind of evaluation that my staff and I give provides one good model. Let me describe what that looks and feels like.

If you bring your child to my office for an evaluation, we will first try to get to know you and your child. In the increasingly impersonal and technology-driven world of medicine, what matters most—the human connection—often gets drowned in a sea of paperwork, tests, and hurried conversations that leave you feeling misunderstood and frustrated. We don't want that to happen, and you should not tolerate that happening. Wherever you go for help, insist on being heard. Don't let your child or yourself become an inhuman, moveable part in the faceless machine of modern medicine. The best kind of help for you or your child begins not with a test or a checklist but with a conversation. It always begins with a genuine, human connection. It begins with the person from whom you are seeking help inviting you to speak and to tell of the details of your life. It always begins in what the poet Yeats called the rag-and-bone shop of the heart.

Find a doctor—or social worker, psychologist, or counselor—who first of all wants to know you and your child. Find someone who can smile and who can listen and who can laugh. Find someone who isn't in too much of a rush, even if he or she is busy. Find someone who wants to learn from you about your life, not just tell you what's wrong with you or your child and what you should do. One of the most powerful therapeutic elements in all of medicine is also one of the most rapidly disappearing: the human connection between the person offering help and the person seeking it.

For example, if you come to one of my offices, we will help you relax so you can be open and real and tell us your full story. We will try not to hurry you. We will talk with you and your child, review teachers' comments and other school records, take a look at medical records, and probably do some brief neuropsychological testing as well. Contrary to popular belief, there is no single test for ADD, so we rely on a comprehensive, broad-based evaluation. During the process we will likely laugh quite a bit—stories from the land of ADD tend to be quite funny—and we will encourage you to laugh, too, as humor is one of the best antidotes to the distress ADD can cause. But there will also be boxes of tissues around should tears fall, as they often do. Like laughter, tears are also good; they are part of the true and full story. All in all, the process should be interesting, enjoyable, relieving, and infused with hope. Whoever evaluates your child should also listen to *you,* the parent. A parent's gut can tell us a lot; a parent's intuition is immensely valuable.

"The best advice I got from another mom with a child with AD/HD was that moms know their child better than anyone. She said that if what a physician was doing to or for your child or for the parents didn't feel right, it probably wasn't. She said that doctors are like teachers in that there are some great ones and some really awful ones."

—Marlene, mother of a child with ADD

Once the evaluation is complete, I will invite you into my office to discuss what we have found. Anyone delivering the news of an ADD diagnosis to you should be as sensitive and careful as in the scenario I describe below. The first time a child hears that his brain works differently, he should hear it in a way that does not discourage or denigrate him. There are many ways to do this, but I offer the following as one example. I have various colleagues who have developed their own individual ways, all of them excellent. What we all share is the desire to present the information in such a way that hope is kindled, not extinguished. Here's my way of doing it—certainly not the only way, but one way.

A Strength-Based Delivery of an ADD Diagnosis to a Child

Sam, age ten, is sitting in a chair in my office, with his parents on either side of him.

I begin, "Well, Sam, we've gotten to know you a bit, and I've talked about you with the other people you've spoken to today." Sam, baseball cap on backward, is looking at the rug on the floor. "I want to tell you that I have great news for you and your parents." Now Sam looks up. This is not what he was expecting to hear. "You have an awesome brain. You have a Ferrari race car for a brain. Do you know what a Ferrari is?"

Sam nods and says, "I made a model of one."

"Well, then you know that a Ferrari is an incredibly fast race car. It wins lots of races. And with your brain, you are going to win lots of races. You are so lucky. You have a turbocharged brain."

Sam smiles. His parents smile as well.

"But there's one problem. You have bicycle brakes. Your brakes aren't strong enough to control your race car brain. So you can't stop when you see a stop sign or slow down when you come into a curve. When you want to concentrate, often you can't, and when you are bored, often you can't keep yourself from drifting off or acting up."

Sam's parents laugh and Sam nods.

"Well, I'm a brake specialist. I'm here to help you strengthen your brakes so you can slow down when you need to. That way you can win races instead of spinning out when you go around curves or crashing into someone else when you run through a stop sign."

In fact, a race car brain with defective brakes is quite an accurate representation of the neurology of ADD. Russell Barkley, one of the great researchers in the field of ADD, conceptualizes ADD as a state of relative disinhibition. The inhibitory circuits in the brain fail to work properly. This leads to the three core symptoms of ADD, what Barkley calls the holy trinity of ADD: distractibility, impulsivity, and restlessness or hyperactivity. The inability to inhibit stimuli coming in from the outside world leads to distractibility and the intermittent lack of focus that so plagues people with ADD. The inability to inhibit impulses that originate inside a person leads to the impulsive and hyperactive behaviors that get people with ADD into so much trouble. Therefore, most treatments aim to improve a person's ability to voluntarily inhibit activity in the brain.

As I see it, that's just a fancy medical way of saying that you have a race car brain with faulty brakes. You can't put the brakes on when you need to, and this can cause major problems in life. If you can't stop, you can't focus. If you can't focus, you can't do well at anything.

I explain all this to Sam and his parents. I can see by the looks on their faces that it makes sense to them, but I can also see that they have some reservations.

"The world will tell you that you have attention deficit disorder, or ADD, but I want you to think of it as a race car brain with weak brakes. I don't want you to think of it as a disorder, but rather as a potential gift, a gift that can be hard to unwrap. As you've already learned, life with ADD can be really tough, and you can feel like ADD is a curse and not in the least bit a gift. But if you work hard and get the right help, you will find that the gift gradually gets unwrapped. Then you'll see how lucky you are."

"Could you tell us more about the gift part?" his mother asks, her voice conveying both hope and skepticism. After all, considering the multitude of problems ADD has created in Sam's life so far, where exactly are the signs of a gift? It makes me think of the old joke about the eternal optimist, the punch line of which is, "With all this manure, there's gotta be a pony somewhere!" Life with ADD can produce a lot of manure, to be sure. But there is a pony.

"Sure," I reply. "Based on the intake interview we did with Sam, let me take a stab at describing what Sam is like on a day-to-day basis.

"My guess is that Sam is a highly imaginative kid with a real knack for thinking outside the box. In fact, he may have trouble thinking inside the box! I bet he is fun-loving and has a special, sometimes zany sense of humor. I bet he is highly intuitive and often comes up with solutions to problems without knowing where they came from and comes up with ideas without knowing how he thought of them. I bet he has a special quality that draws people in, a kind of charisma even, and I bet you worry that this special quality is at risk for getting destroyed by all the criticisms and rebukes he receives. I bet he never gives up. I bet as many times as he gets punished or put down, he still keeps coming back for more. I bet he's tenacious. Do you know what *tenacious* means, Sam?"

Sam shakes his head.

"It means you never give up. It means no matter how

many times you get told you can't, you still try. This probably annoys your mom quite a bit when she is telling you
you're not allowed to do something and you keep pestering her trying to make her give in. And your mom is right,
pestering is annoying, and you need to learn not to do that
to your mom, but your tenacity—and now you know what
the word means—can also be a great asset in your life. You
know what *asset* means—it means an advantage, which
ADD can certainly be."

I go on. "What else makes ADD an advantage in dis-
guise? Energy. Curiosity. Creativity. Some experts say these
qualities are no higher in people with ADD than in the general population, but my experience tells me that they are.
And the more you notice them and nourish them, the stronger they become.

"Let's see. What else is good? A tendency to forgive.
People with ADD can't remember a grudge long enough
to hold one. A tendency to be big-hearted and generous. A
tendency to be highly sensitive, to the point of being easily
hurt. A tendency to surprise people with sudden unexpected
insights. For example, one day my daughter, who has the gift
of ADD, said to me, 'Dad, what we need is a world where
no one holds back in life out of fear.' We had been talking
about 9/11. She was thirteen years old at the time. I have no
idea where she came up with that, but it is an insight I relish and refer to often. This is what kids—and adults—with
ADD tend to do: surprise you with their insights, talents,
and strengths." I then ask the parents, "How much of this
sounds like Sam?"

"Almost all of it," his mother says. "And what worries

me so much is what you also said, that all the good parts will get lost under all the negative criticisms he has had to deal with. Not just from school, but from me, too."

As is almost always the case with parents of kids who have ADD, Sam's mom is a wonderful mom. It is only natural that she gets frustrated with him now and then and becomes critical. She hasn't known what was really going on. I say to her, "It can be unbelievably difficult being the parent of a child with ADD, *especially* before you have it diagnosed. That's why today is a good-news day. You all are finding out what's been going on and what to do about it. What to do about it won't be easy, but life should get considerably better for you all from now on."

"But what about the long term?" the mom asks. "The reason I put off getting this evaluation is that all the bad things I heard about ADD scared me away. What kind of a future do we have to look forward to?"

I look at Sam. "What do you think, Sam? Are you going to win some races?"

Sam smiles and nods. I feel like jumping up and giving him a high five.

The Diagnosis Should Kindle Hope

As I've said, breaking the news to a child that he or she has ADD needs to be done gently, and with an emphasis on the positive. Likewise, the news should be delivered to you with compassion and understanding, but not with sorrow or pity. Any clinician or professional who suggests that a diagnosis of ADD is a curse without any possible positive side to it is someone to walk away from. Acknowledging that ADD can be difficult makes sense, but focusing on the bad outcomes can be hugely damaging at this critical moment.

Of course—and you likely know this already—there are bad outcomes. But the bad outcomes occur when no one knows what's going on and when the right help is not available. Then you get the stories of people getting into trouble with the law, going to prison, getting into drugs, and all the rest. Those things do happen. The prisons are full of people with undiagnosed ADD. People with ADD are more likely to get divorced, be unable to hold down a job, get into trouble with money, and just generally flounder in their lives. Untreated, ADD can be a lifelong ordeal of the worst kind. It is particularly frustrating because the person knows he could do better, but no matter how hard he tries, he keeps coming up short. Disappointment follows disappointment, and after a while the person feels that there's no point in trying. Being tenacious, he keeps trying, and keeps falling short, which leads to problems with anger and sometimes violence and drug abuse. Sometimes the person with ADD does give up. Sometimes he falls into a terrible depression. Sometimes he commits suicide. But while we all need to understand these associated risks, an initial evaluation is simply *not* the time to describe the details of the downside. To the contrary, now's the time to ignite hope. So I go on to say, "With the right kind of help, Sam is going to win plenty of races. Sam will lead a wonderful life. We just need to make sure he gets the right kind of help."

As a parent reading this book, you've clearly come looking for the "right kind of help." As I've said earlier, above all, you need to love your child as he is. You need to make sure *he* knows that you love him for who he is. Of course, this is not a one-time thing; expressing unconditional love is an ongoing process.

And don't feel bad about those times when you lose your cool and overreact. All of us parents do this, most of us many times. The one rule I would urge you to observe is never to hit your child. No hitting is a good policy for all households to subscribe to. Hitting is never necessary, and it is often destructive. A generation ago spanking was routine. Today it ought to be obsolete. We ought to have progressed beyond it. Anyone can hit a child. What takes skill and patience is not hitting a child.

Having said that, there will be times when you lose your temper, scream and yell, and are tempted to hit. This is completely normal. It doesn't mean you don't love your child. It is simply evidence that you are human, and raising kids is taxing. So go easy on yourself. After you lose it, apologize to your child. Your apology serves as a good model for those times when you ask your child to apologize.

Often the next issue discussed in an evaluation meeting will be the medications that might help your child. Of all the treatments we have, medication provides the quickest and most dramatic improvement. Medication doesn't always work, though, and many parents don't want to try it. A good clinician and/or evaluator will not push medications on your child. You should never be told that you *must* give them to your child. That said, the time may well come when you'll want to.

Due to lack of education, most people harbor unnecessary fears about stimulant medications such as Concerta and Adderall, the two most commonly prescribed medications for ADD. Even though from a medical standpoint they are very safe and effective when prescribed properly, most people have heard so many negatives about them that they fear them. The way we both describe the benefits of prescription medication is that when it works, it works like a pair of eyeglasses. It doesn't make you smarter or more compliant; it simply allows you to focus your mind more sharply, which in turn allows you to use your God-given talents more effectively.

> "Get educated. Don't listen to only one person. Don't rely only on medication, and don't refuse to try it."
> —Allison, mother of a child with ADD

> "Without a doubt, connecting with other parents who have children with ADD is what has made the biggest difference in our handling of the situation—the problems we face as a family. It was great to be able to hear how they had all used different strategies that could be used with my son. I realized that I was not a bad parent and that I was not alone. I found other moms who were going through the same thing."
> —Marlene, mother of a child with ADD

On the other hand, medication can be overprescribed. Not only the stimulants (such as Concerta, Ritalin, Vyvanse, and Adderall) but also other categories of medications (such as Strattera, antidepressants, antianxiety agents, and antipsychotic medications) can be prescribed too freely, especially in the current system and culture, which favor "quick-fix" interventions. Medication can work quickly. However, it is not always effective, and it can do damage if not used properly. For more on this, see chapter 13 or my book *Delivered from Distraction*.

The point to remember here is that you should never give your child medication until you feel comfortable doing so. The medication won't work nearly as well if you—and your child—are afraid of taking it, anyway. And there are many interventions we can offer other than medication. We've already stated the most important, which is to understand ADD as a potential gift. Not everyone sees it this way, of course. We think the reason it has taken time to promote this model is that ADD can be such a burden and such a curse. It can wear families out. It can lead to huge struggles in families, daily fights, even divorce. To call it a potential gift can seem absurd if your whole life is being torn apart by ADD gone out of control.

But we have seen many times over our years of working with people who have ADD that a strength-based model gets much better results than a model that emphasizes problems and disabilities. It only makes common sense. But you'd be amazed at how many kids with ADD spend a whole day in school and never hear one word of approval or praise. They only hear words of reprimand, redirection, or remediation. Can you imagine how you'd feel if your entire day at work was spent being told about the various ways in which you fall short, then doing exercises to get better at what you're bad at? You'd feel a lot better about it if you were reminded now and then that there's a pot of gold at the end of the rainbow, that you have some special talents, and that all this hard work is going to pay off in some exciting ways. Using a strength-based model will illuminate that pot of gold for your child and maximize the chances of his finding it one day.

Chapter 5

From Moral to Deficit-Based to Strength-Based Thinking

I once received the following e-mail:

> *What would you recommend as an advocacy state-ment/response to others who speak so negatively about ADHD, obviously not understanding the "gift"? My specific examples are the recent responses of two very educated people, one a heart surgeon and the other a teacher, for heaven's sake. When I mentioned my children's ADHD to my friend the surgeon, his response was a very sympathetic "I'm so sorry," as if I had just told him that my children were terminally ill. The teacher didn't know of my family history—she was speaking in general about kids in class—and her comment "Some kids are sur-rounded by ADHD wackos" almost made me fall out of my chair. I said nothing and later regretted that I didn't speak up as an advocate to educate both of these people that ADHD is nothing to be sorry for and certainly does not make one a "wacko." Do*

you have a one-liner, a common response, to people
who are so uninformed about ADHD?

I don't have a one-liner. The stakes are too high for sound-bite explanations. This is not merely a matter of nomenclature or semantics. Nor is it a dry, academic debate. It's a matter of doing what's best for our children, not to mention the adults who have ADD as well. As long as street wisdom considers children with ADD to be "wackos" and their parents to be in need of the kind of sympathy that's usually reserved for when someone is terminally ill, we will continue to misunderstand and mistreat those who have this wonderfully interesting, potentially valuable trait.

To understand how we got to where we are today, take a quick look back. It turns out that our traditions in mental health are anything but healthy.

For most of human history, problems related to the mind—that is to say, problems related to learning, emotion, thought, or behavior—were viewed through the lens of morality. If you were a child who misbehaved, your diagnosis was that you were "bad"—a moral diagnosis, indeed a judgment. If not bad, then you were wayward, miscreant, or incorrigible. In fact, the blatantly moral term *incorrigible* appeared in textbooks of pediatric medicine well into the twentieth century.

Theology also wormed its way in. Free will was its admission ticket. If a child did not obey his parents or his teachers, it was judged that he had *chosen* not to, that he was not trying hard enough to do what was right. He was, therefore, sinning. People regarded the child's soul as a proving ground in a contest between God and the devil. It was up to the parent—or teacher, or other person in charge of the child—to "assist" God and the child in the struggle with the devil by beating the devil out of the child. Hence we see the vast and vicious history of child abuse through the millennia committed, cruelly and paradoxically enough, in the name of God.

At the center of the moral model lay the notion that free will controlled all learning, emotion, and behavior. People clutched at the idea that free will controlled everything as tightly as they once held to the notion that the earth sat at the center of the solar system. Just as it was reassuring to believe that earth held center stage in the solar system, it was reassuring to believe that free will gave a person control over his emotions, learning, behavior, and thought. All he needed to do was try hard enough and his problems would be solved.

According to the moral model, a model that still captures the imagination of many an otherwise enlightened adult, all a child had to do to behave was *intend* to behave. To overcome depression, all a person had to do was intend to; in other words, all the person had to do was cheer up. To learn a difficult subject, all a student had to do was apply himself diligently to the task. Free will ruled; hard work conquered all.

The moral model tortured children and adults alike. Adults who suffered from what we would now diagnose as depression or bipolar disorder were "diagnosed" as failures in the contest between God and the devil, which is to say that they were thought to be possessed. Their "treatment" was confinement, execution, or both. Children who did not do what adults commanded them to do were simply beaten repeatedly, with more and more vigor, if good results did not ensue. If a parent lacked the stomach to beat his child, wise elders counseled him on the necessity of doing so. After all, the child's soul was at stake. Spare the rod and spoil the child. That was all the license the moral model needed to justify centuries of castigation.

On a psychological level, this was all quite understandable. Since people had no idea how to help people with mental difficulties, they did what people always do when they feel helpless: they blamed the person who made them feel helpless. Then they punished that person. If you were a child, you got harsh beatings. You ran away as soon as you could. If you were an adult, you were shackled to a stone wall in a dungeon or prison. On Sundays and holidays, you'd be brought outdoors and put on display. This is how a happy, normal eighteenth-century family might spend a frolicsome Sunday afternoon: start by watching the lunatics on display as they drooled, talked to themselves, twisted, and screamed, then cap the fun off by attending a public execution.

Toward the end of the eighteenth century a few people began to say no to such treatment. In 1793, a great man changed the course of the treatment of the mentally ill forever. Philippe Pinel ordered the chains removed from the insane housed at his institution, the Hospice de Bicêtre in Paris. It is appalling to think that he faced opposition, but he did. People preferred their lunatics chained up (many still do today). But Pinel prevailed, and the "moral model" of condemning and torturing those who suffer from mental problems began to crumble. Its remnants persist to this day in the form of stigma, ignorance, and prejudice against the mentally ill, but the destructive influence of the moral model diminishes each year.

In this country, Benjamin Rush, now hailed as the father

of American psychiatry, pioneered the humane treatment of the mentally ill. Working at the Pennsylvania Hospital in Philadelphia, this brilliant man, who was also a signer of the Declaration of Independence and a leader in the effort to free slaves, brought the practices of Pinel to the United States. He insisted that doctors should try to understand mental patients as people, not as primitive beasts possessed by evil spirits. He urged physicians to "catch the patient's eye and look him out of countenance. Be always dignified. Never laugh at or with them. Be truthful. Meet them with respect. Act kindly towards them in their presence." It is just as I said before: the best treatment always begins in a respectful, human connection.

As doctors began to approach mental issues not as moral or spiritual failings but as biological conditions, like heart or kidney failure, some bizarre treatments emerged. One such, the "whirling chair," was invented by Rush. Rush would place his patient in a chair that was then made to rotate around a central axis, generating such centripetal force that it would induce unconsciousness or even cerebral hemorrhage in the patient. If the doctor discerned blood emanating from the patient's ear, he stopped the whirling of the chair, the session of "treatment" complete. It's not clear what the rationale for this treatment was, other than that it was considered "tranquilizing." My hunch is that even a man as humane as Rush could feel frustrated by the stubbornly obstreperous behavior of a patient out of control. I think Rush used the chair not just to treat the patient but to take his own anger out on him as well. The "moral" retributive model of taking your frustrations out against the person who frustrates you never completely disappears, not even in as sweet and enlightened a man as Rush, not even in you, and certainly not in me.

Still, as horrific as it was, the whirling chair and other body-based treatments did indicate progress, the beginnings of what we now call the medical model. Working in the medical model, Rush was not an inquisitor attacking the weak will of a miscreant but a *doctor* treating a *patient* suffering from a *disease*. Even though the treatment was painful and ineffective, that it was seen as a treatment for a disease represented a radical shift away from the moral model. The patient was put in the whirling chair not to motivate him to try harder but to help him recover from a disease over which he had no control. No longer was willpower seen as the sole change agent for all problems related to learning, emotion, thought, and behavior.

The medical model disturbed—and still disturbs—many people for the same reason that Copernicus disturbed people when he claimed that the earth did not sit supreme at the center of the solar system. It is far more comforting to believe that all a person has to do is want to behave in order to behave, want to learn in order to learn, and want to be happy in order to be happy.

But the medical model took root against vitriolic, impassioned opposition because science and human decency were on its side. All the evidence pointed to the fact that hard work and willpower, while always important, did not tell the whole story.

Applying the medical model to what we now call ADD, people began to entertain the idea that hard work could not provide the full and definitive solution to the struggles these disruptive children faced. Beatings had failed. For thousands of years, people kept trying beatings and moral lectures because that's all they could think of and because they were encouraged to do so. But when people such as Pinel and Rush started urging a more understanding approach, a more medical viewpoint, children started to benefit. Instead of just being consigned to euphemistically named "reform schools," children with what we now call ADD found their way into hospitals.

In 1937 at one such hospital—what is now Bradley Hospital in Providence, Rhode Island—the treatment of ADD was forever changed. Dr. Charles Bradley, a distant relative of the person after whom the hospital was named, decided to try something altogether new to treat ADD. Boys who might have been diagnosed as incorrigible in the old moral model now found medical sanctuary in the wise and innovative hands of Dr. Bradley and his staff.

Bradley didn't know what caused the boys to be so hyperactive, but he knew it wasn't just a lack of discipline or a failure of the will. So he worked with these boys, trying one behavioral intervention after another—much as we do today. He defied society's conventional wisdom by insisting that they needed medical treatment for an as yet poorly understood disease. He identified the problem as neurological, not moral.

Being willing to try whatever worked, as long as it was safe and legal (the same principle that guides what is offered in this book), Bradley hit upon the idea of giving the boys Benzedrine, an amphetamine (or what is called "speed" in common parlance). Others in the hospital were given the drug to combat headaches resulting from treatments for other conditions, and Bradley noticed behavioral changes in them and thought the medication might help the hyperactive boys.

I would love to have seen the look on the face of Dr. Bradley's head nurse when he announced that he wanted to try speed on these out-of-control boys. The nurse must have thought old Bradley had finally gone round the bend. If the head nurse was spunky, as most are, I imagine that the dialogue might have gone like this:

Bradley: I think we ought to try Benzedrine on these boys. It's good for the headaches the others have. Maybe it will be good for these boys and their overactive behavior.

Nurse: Really? I can't imagine why. I don't mean to speak out of turn, Dr. Bradley, but have you gone mad? Giving these boys Benzedrine would be like throwing kerosene on a fire. I know these boys can be exasperating, but I don't think we ought to totally throw caution to the wind!

Bradley: No, I have not gone mad. And I'll thank you not to suggest that again.

Nurse: I'm sorry, Dr. Bradley, but this idea just seems insane to me.

Bradley: There you go again, telling me I'm crazy. I am not insane. At least I don't think so. Perhaps I should thank you for raising the possibility. I know my wife would. Still, I want to give it a try. I've seen it change the behavior of the ones who take it for headaches.

Nurse: These boys have more than headaches! They may be headaches to us, but they don't suffer from headaches. Please. Your idea makes no sense at all.

Bradley: Many new ideas make no sense at first. And what if I'm right, but we don't give it a try? How long do these boys have to wait for someone to take a chance and try something new?

Nurse: You should try something new if it makes even a tiny bit of sense. But this doesn't make even the tiniest bit of sense. As I said, it's like trying to put out a fire by pouring kerosene on it. If we should take a chance just for the sake of taking a chance, why not try horse manure on them, or moonbeams?

Bradley: I want to try the Benzedrine. If I'm wrong, you can tell people you did your best to talk me out of it. You can even tell people I'm insane, if you'd like to.

Nurse: All right, all right. If you insist. But I can't take responsibility for what happens.

Bradley: Of course not. But just think, it might work.

It did work, and better than manure or moonbeams. It was all but miraculous. In one of the great breakthroughs not only in the history of the treatment of ADD but also in the history of our understanding of the mind, twenty minutes after taking the medication the boys were able to sit still and study. Not only did they not object, they loved how the medication helped them. They hadn't enjoyed being out of control any more than the staff had. They so liked Benzedrine that they called it the "arithmetic pill," because it allowed them to concentrate and learn their math facts, among other tasks.

In twenty minutes a medical intervention succeeded where thousands of years of beatings had failed. In twenty minutes a pill did what nothing else had been able to do: give these boys the ability to work up to their potential.

After that, the medical model was here to stay. The medical model shone light into the dungeon of the moral model, freeing not only children but adults as well from the shackles of condemnation, ridicule, and punishment. While the moral model persists even today in the form of stigma and prejudice against those who struggle with mental differences, it does not plant its heavy boot upon people's necks the way it used to. Now, thanks to the medical model, we seek to *treat a disease* rather than reform a moral failing. The difference is mammoth in its impact.

When people propose new treatments today and face stern rebukes simply for proposing something new, I think of Dr. Bradley and his courage in veering away from accepted treatments. And Bradley's example is the rule, not the exception. If you look at the history of medicine, one of the lessons that bites you like a viper is that if you have a new idea, beware! You will be vilified, excommunicated, defrocked, and despised before your new idea becomes accepted. It has been observed that new ideas are first ridiculed, then despised, then embraced as obvious. Nowhere is that more true than in the history of medicine.

Pinel, Rush, Bradley, and many others tore down the

moral model and replaced it with a biologically based, empirically tested medical model for understanding differences of the mind. The mind and the body gradually got reunited, after millennia of a tumultuous and destructive separation.

We have all benefited. Not only do medical treatments work far better than moral ones, but the medical model combats stigma and prejudice with reason and understanding. While it is still the case that many people who could get help from a mental-health professional refuse to do so out of fear based on stigma and prejudice, the trend is toward reason and acceptance. This is all due to the power of science and education. We have a lot of work yet to do, but we are getting there. Someday, probably not in my lifetime but with luck in my children's lifetimes, we will look at the stigma and prejudice regarding mental differences with the same shock and disdain that we now look at racial or religious stigma and prejudice.

"The school nurse told us that our child just needed some good spankings. Even my in-laws suggested minor beatings! We were also told that he behaved this way because he was eating sugar, or because of the dyes in his food. All blamed me, Mom, for not punishing him or for not being smart enough to feed him well, in spite of the fact that I have a home economics degree and studied child development and nutrition. Everyone seemed to be an expert, but none of them made any positive suggestions that could help."

—Marlene, mother of a son with ADD

The Deficit in the Deficit-Based Model

For all its benefits, however, the medical, deficit-based model creates problems. As much as it broke the chains that shackled the insane, it now inadvertently forges new chains. These chains are invisible but crippling nonetheless. They are chains of shame, fear, loss of hope, and lowered expectations.

The medical model is built upon a model of what's wrong. It is built on a model of pathology. You go to the doctor because you feel sick, not because you feel well. You don't say to yourself, *I feel great today—I think I'll call my doctor.*

It is your doctor's job to tell you what's wrong with you and how you can take care of what's wrong. Your doctor— and I am one myself—trains for a decade or so after college just to be able to tell you what's wrong with you and to know how to fix it. Your doctor gets very little training in health, in what's right, because that's not why you go to see a doctor.

Therefore, when you get a medical diagnosis, it tells you what's wrong with you, and stops there. When the diagnosis is of the kidney or the heart, that's all right. But when the diagnosis pertains to the mind, that's much trickier, and sometimes even dangerous.

When we tell a person that he has a disease of the mind— be it depression, ADD, bipolar disorder, anxiety disorder, or any of the diagnoses we make in psychiatry—it might seem as though we are telling that person that he himself is impaired. We personally identify with our brains and minds. We do not do that with any other organ.

The medical diagnosis of the mind therefore risks creating new disorders, the disorders we've cited, such as shame, fear, inferiority, loss of hope, reduced enthusiasm, shattered dreams, and despair. No doctor creates these on purpose, of course, but that makes the creating of them all the more insidious. Implicit in the medical/psychiatric diagnosis is an alienating attribution of the patient's fundamental impairment and social unacceptability. We have get-well cards for people with all manner of physical illness, from cancer to heart attacks to broken legs. But we have never seen a get-well card that read "Hope your depression lifts soon!" or "Hope those hallucinations go away fast!" or "Hope your mania subsides quickly this time around!" or "Thinking of you as you wrestle with ADD."

The inadvertent damage done by the medical diagnosis can be repaired by using a strength-based model. Instead of telling a person that he suffers from ADD, tell him, as I imagined telling Sam earlier, that he has a race car brain with weak brakes. (You can apply this approach to all diagnoses of the mind. For example, tell a person who has depression that this condition is a marker of talent, as indeed it is, and that while the depression hurts, once it is controlled the underlying talents can be developed and used. Or tell a person who suffers from bipolar disorder that this condition also carries with it considerable talents most of the time. Tell a person who suffers from addictions that once the addiction is under control, the next step is tapping into the talents the addiction was concealing. Indeed, the addicted population is one of our most talented groups. If you doubt that, just go to an AA meeting.)

The key is to make the strength the headline and the problem the subhead. The medical model does it in reverse. It states the problem as the headline, and the strengths get mentioned only in footnotes.

Far from being simply semantic, this difference is profound in its impact upon the child and the family. If you tell a parent that her daughter has a gift that's hard to unwrap, that makes a radically different impact than if you tell a parent that her daughter has a mental disorder in need of treatment.

The first way of putting it brings hope, enthusiasm, and positive energy into the room. The second way expels those forces from the room. Not on purpose, of course, but many doctors send their newly diagnosed patients back to their cars in tears. Being freshly diagnosed with a mental illness or having your child so diagnosed does not feel good. Indeed, it can be traumatizing.

"I found that learning about the diagnosis of ADD was one of the most liberating experiences of my entire life. I can now manage my reactions, my emotions, and my life with a clear understanding of underlying motivations when I stray from my structure and my goals. As you put it, it's a blessing and not a curse. As I see it in my five-year-old son, I see the same characteristics that made my early childhood and teenage years so much fun. He and I have already started talking about our 'special gift' and how we can use it to achieve anything we want."

—Robert, an adult with ADD

It is time to move beyond the medical model and embrace a strength-based model. In so doing, we can avoid creating crippling disorders such as shame, fear, loss of hope, and broken dreams. These do more damage than ADD. But they can be avoided. Simply identify strengths, talents and possible talents, interests and possible interests, potential strengths, hopes, dreams, enthusiasms, desires, and wishes as soon as possible. Shine a light on those. Let that illuminated landscape fill your child's mind—and yours.

If you do that, you will be infinitely more able—and eager—to tackle the problems ADD can present. You and your child can be unstoppable in your pursuit of all that your child is capable of achieving.

Chapter 6

Emphasizing the Positive—in Action

No one can be as convincing as the parent, child, or family that is living out the experience of unwrapping the gifts embedded in ADD. In the story that follows, written by Daniel's mom, you will see the power of the strength-based model as opposed to a model that emphasizes what's defective or disabled.

Daniel's Story

Our son Daniel showed signs of ADD at a very young age. When he entered preschool, my husband and I were advised by his teacher that Daniel was having difficulty staying on task. Her observation was that, in all likelihood, Daniel had ADD but it was too early to do any level of evaluation. Her advice was to be aware as Daniel went forward.

Through his kindergarten years, we continued to hear how easily Daniel was distracted while in class. It was not a surprise when we received a call from Daniel's first-grade teacher on the second day of school to let us know that she was concerned about his distractibility. His teacher suggested that we proceed with testing. The school district conducted the testing, which confirmed what had been a concern for over two years: Daniel had ADD. The first thing the school psychologist did, in a very somber manner, was to hand me a book to read. She was almost apologetic in her approach, as if she had just advised me that Daniel had a terminal disease. I immediately sat down to read the book, which began on page one by describing ADD as "minimal brain dysfunction." I could not believe what I was reading. My son seemed so bright, and yet this book described brain abnormalities seen on scans of ADD children. I closed the book and returned it to the psychologist. As a registered nurse, I knew it was time to become educated on ADD by leading experts in the field who could help my son, rather than listen to generalists from a school district portray him in a manner that would make him an outcast with his friends and peers.

Within weeks, I attended a conference on ADD hosted by Dr. Edward Hallowell, who introduced himself as having both ADD and dyslexia. Dr. Hallowell's explanation of ADD was 180 degrees away from the clinical description offered in the book I had previously been given by the school psychologist. In fact, the information I learned during the first half of the conference led me to call my husband at work, excited to tell him that our son's diagnosis was not as hopeless as we had been led to believe, and that he would be fine.

We soon scheduled an appointment for Daniel to be seen by Dr. Hallowell. During the initial ten minutes of the meeting, Daniel was busy creating a building out of Legos. I recall Dr. Hallowell saying, "Clearly this child is bright and

creative; just look at what he built and explained to me."
Dr. Hallowell immediately turned his attention to Daniel.
He asked Daniel some basic questions about how things
went for him in school.

"Do you like school, Dan?"

"Yes," said Daniel.

"Do you sometimes find it hard to be in class?"

"Yes," said Daniel.

"Do you ever forget things when you are in class?"
asked Dr. Hallowell.

"Yes," said Daniel.

This line of questioning continued with Daniel answer-
ing each question while still working on his Lego creation.
Dr. Hallowell then asked Daniel if he could put down the
Legos for a few minutes so they could talk. Daniel was only
too willing to oblige.

Dr. Hallowell went on to explain to Daniel that he had
a "supercharged brain," which was working so fast that it
caused him to sometimes forget where he put his pencil, what
it was his teacher wanted him to do, or other similar simple
but important tasks in class. Daniel was now completely mes-
merized by what he was hearing. Dr. Hallowell asked Daniel
if he would be willing to take some medicine for his "super-
charged brain"—and Dan said he was willing to try it. The
medicine Daniel would take (Concerta) was like "oil for your
brain." As Dr. Hallowell explained, "It will slow things down
and allow you to focus better and even remember where you
put things." Daniel was excited by what he was hearing,
especially when he heard that his brain was "special."

After we conferred with his pediatrician, Daniel began
to take the Concerta. The benefits were immediate. His

reading skills, which had been one to two grade levels below his peers, improved a full grade level within a couple of months. According to his teacher, his ability to focus in class improved significantly. Above all, Daniel could not wait to share with everyone who would listen about his "supercharged brain"! He let the world know that his brain was special, which made him *special. Sure, he had to take medicine, the oil that helped his supercharged brain, but that was okay; it helped him in school and everywhere else.*

Daniel had always been bothered by his feeling of how people thought about him. But after learning about his special brain, Daniel's self-esteem shot up off the charts. He looked at everything in his life with optimism. He now knew that if he took his medicine, his supercharged brain would only get better. At one point in class, Daniel told his teacher he was doing his best because "he had a supercharged brain and she didn't." This was the same teacher who'd impressed upon us that Daniel needed to be tested. Some teachers might have taken Daniel's comments as a sign that Daniel was being a wise guy. Instead, she smiled, knowing Daniel was just proud of his newfound skills. As parents, this teacher is a hero in our minds, and someday Daniel will know how much of a hero she was, too.

Daniel's positive ADD story continues today. His teachers remark regularly about his positive attitude and his willingness to share with all who want to know that he has ADD. Teachers marvel at his self-esteem. This year for the first school open house, the students were asked to write an autobiographical poem. Daniel's began with "smart, athletic, and handsome" to describe himself. Oftentimes other parents are shocked when they learn that Dan has

ADD, something we openly, almost proudly declare whenever the opportunity presents itself. Part of the reason they are surprised is because many children with ADD have low self-esteem because they are continually told that they have something wrong with them. Dan, however, has healthy self-esteem that has developed from the positive attitude of the people around him in regard to ADD. We continually allow Dan to grow and mature by helping him see that all parts of him are special, including his ADD.

Daniel also tells his friends about ADD. He can sometimes be heard telling his friends while they are creating something at play that he can "think outside the box" or that his brain is "supercharged like a race car." He recently shared his story with a friend and his mother. The mother called me to say she was amazed at how open and positive Daniel was about having ADD. She had concerns about her own son possibly having ADD. After listening to Daniel, this mother no longer felt the negative stigma that so often accompanies ADD. Instead she is now looking into how to improve things for her son in the same manner Daniel enjoys. Daniel is now both a student who has ADD and a poster child for how ADD is an asset when treated properly.

As Daniel gets older, the impact of ADD on his life evolves. His supercharged-brain stories are legendary in our family and with close friends as well. Daniel has taken complete control over treating his ADD, including making sure he takes his medicine on a daily basis. When he forgets, at some point in the late hours of the morning Daniel will let us all know that he forgot his "brain pill" and we might be in for a "long day." We all laugh, knowing he is *right. We recently went for a Sunday brunch at about 11:30 A.M. Daniel was eating as if he had been on a secluded island for months. We were all staring at him in amazement, since when he properly medicates, his appetite is more subdued. Daniel witnessed us all staring in amazement at how much he was eating, and paused for just a second to declare, "Oops, I forgot my brain pill; my supercharged brain is really hungry!" The laughter was incredible.*

Just five years ago, our son was looked upon as a kid who was out of control and whom many did not want to be around. Today, he is growing into a young man who excels in school, extracurricular activities, and sports. He is admired by teachers, parents, peers, and many others for how positive he is about a condition other students and parents consider an unfair plight imposed upon them for life. Most of all, Daniel is a source of pride to himself and his family for applying his "supercharged brain" in a way that only he can. He still reminds us all on a regular basis that he has the supercharged brain and we don't! Daniel is well loved by his family for the spectacular person that he is, making him a true gift that we are all grateful and proud to have each and every day.

Emphasizing the positive is not a superficial practice of little more importance than a smiley face at the end of a note. A parent who emphasizes the positive is not to be confused with a glorified cheerleader. Emphasizing the positive takes a special skill of its own. Doing it right requires you to be observant, perceptive, judicious, and bold. Cheerleading requires only that you jump up and down, wave your arms, and shout. Any able-bodied person can do it. But emphasizing the positive takes special vision and special commitment. The school psychologist who somberly handed Daniel's mom a book on minimal brain dysfunction thought she was doing the right thing when in fact she was doing exactly the wrong thing. She lacked the special vision and commitment of a person who can emphasize the positive, even in the midst of a mess.

You have to be able to see past the messes to the creative mind that created them. You have to see past the missed deadlines, unmade beds, ignored instructions, and offended teachers and perceive the wheels that are turning inside the child's mind, the special way he or she has of seeing life and living it. Daniel's mother is committed to supporting her son's positive view of his "condition"; she helps him daily by reminding him that the phrase *supercharged brain* begins with the word *super*.

When Daniel's mom was given the book describing Daniel's problem as minimal brain dysfunction, she was bold enough to say no to that diagnosis, not out of denial or an unwillingness to accept the truth, but rather out of knowing her son far better than the people making the diagnosis did, and far better than the people who made up the foolish term *minimal brain dysfunction*.

Daniel's mom had the rare strength it takes to buck the experts and insist that her knowledge of her son take precedence over anyone's supposed expertise. She insisted upon recognizing her son's strengths, not just his shortcomings. She didn't deny that there were problems—all children and adults have one or two problems, after all—but she insisted that Daniel's strengths not get overlooked due to the brouhaha over the problems.

This mom was the most crucial element in Daniel's excellent outcome. Had she accepted the diagnosis of minimal brain dysfunction, Daniel would have grown up believing that he was less than the other kids, that he was defective and disabled, that he was special but in a bad way. Instead, Daniel grew up proud of himself, glad to teach others about his supercharged brain, and eager to show the world all his talents and energy.

Daniel's success, like that of so many others, depended upon his family's embracing a strength-based model.

To do this, not only must you see your entire child, but you must also be so committed to emphasizing what is good and strong in your child that you can stand up to Grandma's criticisms, Uncle George's insistence that all your child needs is a good spanking, or the school's repeated dismal warnings that all is about to be lost unless your child gets serious and drinks from the holy grail called discipline. You must be stalwart, your child's never-say-die ally, the one person in the world who always has smiles in your eyes when your child looks back at you, while at the same time you never allow your child to use ADD as an excuse or as a means of lowering sights or giving up.

As Daniel's mother shows us, emphasizing the positive is far more than cheerleading. Emphasizing the positive is an act of both intellect and heart, of both mind and character, of both perception and faith. It is a rare and valuable skill, perhaps the most important skill the parent of a child who has ADD can learn.

Chapter 7

Mirror Traits

WHAT'S GOOD IN WHAT'S BAD

I will never forget a first-grade boy named Henry who came to see me about a decade ago because he had been deemed a conduct problem by his teacher. In our first meeting Henry's mother sat on the two-seat couch I have in my office while Henry sat in the very comfortable chair I used to sit in years ago, before I had a total hip replacement. I have since renamed it the throne, and I encourage the kids who come to see me to sit there. As I stated at the outset, I want to do anything I can to help them feel more comfortable, as a psychiatrist's office usually ranks right up there with a dentist's office or the principal's office as the least-desired destination they can think of.

Henry had black hair, cut like a bowl around his head, and Harry Potter glasses. He enthusiastically checked out the chair like a man taking a test drive. He looked like a future professor who would race cars in his spare time. As he got comfortable, his mother nervously started to relate to me what had happened at school. She was the kind of mom I have come to know and love: anxious, devoted, and quite overwhelmed by the child she has. "I love him," these moms say, "but I never expected this, and I'm not prepared." "She means everything to me," these moms say, "but I'm just not smart enough to stay one step ahead of her."

"You said he was asked to leave class and report to the principal's office?"

"Yes," the mom said, then looked over at her son. "Is it okay to talk about this in front of Henry?"

Looking at Henry, I asked, "What do you think, Henry? Is it okay with you for your mom to tell me this story?"

"Yes," he said. "It's okay."

"Thank you, Henry. And you jump in anytime if there is anything you want to add or if you think your mom got something wrong." Henry nodded and went back to testing different positions in the chair.

"The class had been studying science," Henry's mom explained. "They learned about fire and how fire requires oxygen to burn. It seems advanced to me for first grade, but this teacher and this school like to go fast. In any case, Henry loves science, so this was great as far as he was concerned. Then they learned about outer space and how it is a vacuum, no air, no oxygen, nothing. Then they learned about the sun and how it is a giant ball of fire.

"At that point, without raising his hand, Henry blurted out, 'But how can the sun be a ball of fire if fire needs oxygen and there is no oxygen in outer space because it's a vacuum out there?' Exasperated because Henry had once again interrupted her class without raising his hand, the teacher became angry and sent him to the principal's office. When I met with her she told me blurting things out was a habit he had, and she wanted to break him of it, which is why she sent him out of class. She also suggested that I speak to a professional, which is why I'm here."

I could tell that Henry was now listening intently, even though he wasn't looking at either his mom or me. "Do you know the answer?" I asked.

"The answer to what?" his mom replied.

"Henry's question. How can the sun be a ball of fire if there's no oxygen?"

"No, I don't," the mom replied. She seemed a bit flustered that that's what I focused on, instead of the problem she was presenting to me. "Do you?"

"I bet Henry knows," I replied.

"How'd you know I know?" Henry quickly asked me.

"Because I know that when you're curious you're unstoppable. You weren't going to rest until you found the answer to the question," I replied.

"It's because the sun is like a big chemical-reaction fire and it doesn't need outside oxygen to burn," Henry announced.

"How did you find that out?" his mom asked in astonishment. "You never told me that."

"You never asked," Henry replied with a smile.

"So how did you find out, buddy?" his mom asked.

"Mr. Bowers and I found out together," Henry replied.

"Really?" his mom replied, sounding quite surprised. She looked me and said, "Mr. Bowers is the principal. He's the one who recommended you."

"Did you and Mr. Bowers talk about the sun when you were sent to his office?" I asked.

"Yes," Henry said with a big smile. "He told me I had asked a very interesting question and we had better find out the answer before I left his office. So we Googled fire and sun and stuff like that and we got the answer."

"Did you get a punishment?" I asked.

"Well, Mr. Bowers told me to try not to interrupt Ms. Swan anymore, but he also told me I would get in really *serious* trouble if I ever stopped asking questions."

Thank God for the Henrys of this world, and for the Mr. Bowerses. Unfortunately, there is usually not a Mr. Bowers around to undo the damage a Ms. Swan can do. Usually, the person in Mr. Bowers's role only compounds the damage. Henry was lucky.

There are many Ms. Swans. In fact, many teachers have a bit of Ms. Swan in them, and perhaps they must to do their job. Whether it is right or not, that fact is not going to change, at least not soon. I used to believe that the solution to the problem was to overhaul the education system, but that task will take longer than today's kids and parents have, so I have come to believe that the most practical solution, at least for now, is to teach kids who learn differently and their parents how to manage school effectively, instead of waiting for schools to learn how to teach all kids effectively. (If you'd like to work with your child's teacher or school to effect change, see chapter 11, "What Should You Tell the School?" Or look at Jenifer Fox's book *Your Child's Strengths* or Peter Jensen's book *Making the System Work for Your Child with ADHD*.)

An excellent way to start helping kids to get the most out of school, and life in general, is to adopt a strength-based model. In order to appreciate the strengths inherent in ADD, it is useful to look beyond the deficit-based medical model and discover what I call the "mirror traits" embedded in the condition.

Throughout my training and much of my practice, I, like most doctors, focused on the problematic side of ADD, the traits that were causing difficulty. This only makes sense. We wanted to help these kids by fixing their deficits.

But then, about a decade ago, because of patients like Henry, I began to emphasize what had been in plain view all along, namely, these mirror traits. The mirror traits are simply the positive side of the negative symptoms associated with ADD. By emphasizing the positives, I found that shame, fear, diminished dreams, and the other problems the deficit-based medical model inadvertently caused quickly subsided.

But how can there be something good embedded in something bad? Quite easily. In fact, ADD is full of such paradoxes. For example, take distractibility, the hallmark negative symptom of ADD. Imagine a child named Johnny whose report cards are full of comments like "Johnny can't focus," "Johnny would get better results if he would pay attention more consistently," "Johnny is more interested in what is going on outside the classroom than what is being discussed inside," "Johnny needs to focus his mind more fully on his class work," and so forth. When a student has more of those kinds of comments than other students, we say he "suffers" from distractibility, and he becomes a logical candidate for the diagnosis of ADD.

But think about this tendency to which we so easily assign the negative term *distractibility*. What is distractibility but a turbocharged kind of curiosity? If your mind cannot resist going where enchantment leads it, and if your mind cannot compel itself to stay where it finds nothing of interest going on, is this necessarily bad? It can be bad, to be sure. If you're highly distractible, you may get into a lot of car accidents (and indeed, people with ADD get into far more car accidents than the average person). But on the other hand, your turbocharged curiosity may lead you to look into the nooks and crannies of life where important secrets and great discoveries hide themselves away.

So is this trait good or bad? It all depends. If your distractibility/curiosity leads you to miss the crucial point in chemistry class and you get a bad grade, then distractibility/curiosity has cost you. But if you came up with a brilliant idea on one of your mental excursions that led you to make a sterling contribution to the chemistry class, then your distractibility/curiosity has helped you. The point is that the tendency is, in and of itself, neither good nor bad. If you see it as neither good nor bad, then you will be less inclined to feel ashamed of it and you will be better equipped to master it and put it to good use than if you see it as an entirely negative trait.

By casting the trait in a neutral light and saying it could be good or it could be bad, you avoid the most dangerous of all learning disabilities, which are shame and fear. Shame and fear hold people back in life, indeed cripple them. ADD need not do that. As I have stated before, unwrapped properly, ADD becomes a gift, an ally. But part of unwrapping it is understanding that a given tendency need not be altogether bad, that there can be good in the bad, just as there can be bad in the good.

Consider another cardinal symptom of ADD, impulsivity. When that word is invoked, it is always done so as a pejorative. No one feels proud when he is called "impulsive." The word is used in the context of criticism, even reprimand. "You're so impulsive!" the child (or adult) with ADD hears all the time. "Think before you act; don't act so impulsively." "With you it's always Fire! Aim! Ready! when it should be Ready! Aim! Fire!" "You never think before you speak." "You have no filter on your brain or on your mouth." "I never know *what* you're going to say." These are not words of praise.

So what's the positive, mirror trait of impulsivity? What possible good could come from having a leaky filter on your brain and being at the mercy of your impulses? Could anything of value be embedded in a tendency so universally deplored?

Absolutely. What is creativity but impulsivity gone right? You don't plan to have a creative idea. You don't say to yourself, "It's 10:00 a.m., time for my creative idea of the day," and then come up with it on schedule, like a hen laying an egg. No, creative ideas do not come on schedule. Creative ideas come unbidden and unannounced. They arrive in the middle of the night, they arrive in the shower, they arrive on your tongue or keyboard without your even realizing your brain had thought them up. Creativity depends upon a person's being somewhat disinhibited, which is to say *impulsive*.

That does not mean we should praise a child's every impulsive act. That does not mean we laud a child's impulsively burping on an elevator or impulsively swatting another child or impulsively speaking out of turn in class. But it does mean that we recognize that within the negative trait called impulsivity there resides the positive trait called creativity. It is a grave mistake not to see both the good and the bad. When you recognize the mirror trait, you can describe the tendency in a balanced way, thereby avoiding the ravages of shame and fear, which is what a child comes to feel when he only hears himself described in negative terms.

Go down the list of symptoms of ADD. You can see that each has a mirror trait. Take hyperactivity, the symptom that first defined this condition. It was boys out of control who brought us ADD. Going back to Dr. Bradley in 1937 and even before, doctors have been trying to control behavior that seemed to be out of control, "as if driven by a motor," as the diagnostic manual puts it today. Not only doctors but also parents, teachers, and all those who supervise children have struggled to find effective ways of limiting hyperactive, aggressive, disruptive behavior. *Nothing* gets a child into trouble faster than violent behavior.

So what's the good in being disruptive and out of control? Is there a mirror trait of hyperactivity? Yes. It is called energy. I have ADD with hyperactivity, and I can tell you that at the age of fifty-eight I am grateful indeed for the extra energy I have. When I was seven, it got me into trouble sometimes, but now it is one of my greatest assets. Of course, I needed to learn how to control my behavior. As I tell kids who have ADD, I needed to learn how to strengthen the brakes in order to win races with my race car brain. Until I learned how to control it, to strengthen my brakes, I was liable to spin out on curves and crash into walls.

Describing hyperactivity also as energy, thereby allowing for a good side or a mirror trait, allows me and other people who have ADD with hyperactivity to feel proud rather than ashamed. Instead of identifying ourselves with a mental impairment, we can see ourselves as race cars with brakes that can't always slow us down. That feels far better than being defective, disordered, disabled, or simply bad.

This is not spin control or an effort to paint a rosy picture of a negative scene. It is the start of unwrapping the gifts that the deficit-based model tends to keep forever wrapped.

Here is a list of some negative symptoms associated with ADD along with their mirror traits, their positive, inseparable counterparts.

Negative Trait Associated with ADD ⟶	Accompanying Positive Mirror Trait
Distractible	Curious
Impulsive	Creative
Hyperactive, restless	Energetic
Intrusive	Eager
Can't stay on point	Sees connections others don't
Forgetful	Gets totally into what he or she is doing
Disorganized	Spontaneous
Stubborn	Persistent, won't give up
Inconsistent	Shows flashes of brilliance
Moody	Sensitive

The more you can reframe your child's symptoms in terms of the mirror trait, the more accurate you'll be in describing the totality of your child, rather than just the problematic part. The deficit-based model ignores strengths. This can be disastrous. Ignoring strengths tends to extinguish them or at best not develop them.

This is in no way to deny that there is a potentially disabling side to ADD. There certainly is. As I've stated before, the prisons are full of people with undiagnosed, untreated

ADD, as are the unemployment lines, the drug rehab centers, and the divorce courts. But there is also a gifted side
to ADD; *that* is the side that packs the power to propel a
child or adult who has ADD on to success, even greatness.
In order to tap into that side, you must first know that it
exists. You must learn how to recognize it. Looking for the
mirror traits of the negative symptoms associated with ADD
allows you to do this.

Some people have doubted me when I tell them how
great a life a person with ADD can live. Some people have
accused me of writing fairy tales, embellishing the truth, and
giving parents of children who have ADD false hope. These
people have urged me to paint a darker, and in their view
more accurate, picture than the one I paint, lest I mislead
people into believing there's more good in ADD than there
truly is.

I respect these people and their point of view, because
we're really all on the same side, the side of trying to help
children and their parents. But their emphasis of what can
go wrong *makes* things go wrong. That's the last thing they
intend to do, but the relentless beating of the negative drum
inserts that negative drumbeat into the minds of the kids
who have ADD as well as their parents' minds. Sadly, the
kids and their parents then start marching to the beat of that
drum, the negative drum.

To prove that there is a different way, I teamed up with
a woman named Catherine Corman to write a book relat-
ing true stories of individuals who struggled with ADD as
children only to become happy, successful adults. It is called
Postively ADD.

Catherine was a professor of history at Harvard until

she had triplets, all of whom turned out to have ADD. She left her academic position to devote herself full-time to raising her kids, trying to unwrap their gifts. Writing our book was one of her ways of unwrapping her children's gifts. She knew firsthand how tough life with ADD can be, but she wanted to show her children true stories of success in the world of ADD.

We selected a wide range of people to profile in our book in order to show how diverse a group they represent. Each story proves in its own irrefutable, true way how wrong those people are who insist ADD *must* be a crippling disability, that there is nothing positive about it, and that the future is dim for all who suffer from the condition. A counterexample definitively disproves a hypothesis. And no counterexample in life is as convincing as a true story, a profile of a real person.

The profiles in *Positively ADD* include:

James Carville, political strategist
Scott Eyre, relief pitcher, Chicago Cubs
Carolyn O'Neal, retired school principal
David Neeleman, founder of JetBlue Airlines
Karl Euler, police officer
Heather Long, graduate student, Rhodes scholar
Devin Barclay, professional soccer player, Columbus Crew
Margaret Turano, director, marketing communications, Amicas
Richard Zienowicz, M.D., F.A.C.S., plastic and reconstructive surgeon
Seelan Paramanandam Manickam, musician

Sharon Wohlmuth, Pulitzer Prize–winning
　　photojournalist
Harbhajan Singh Khalsa, yogic healer
Oman Frame, teacher
Clyde Anderson, chairman, Books-a-Million
Jon Bonnell, chef
Linda Pinney, entrepreneur, chief business officer, Asteres
Clarence Page, Pulitzer Prize–winning journalist,
　　Chicago Tribune

The list speaks for itself, as do the stories in the book. We could have included thousands and thousands more. But those we did include prove a point that is vital for all parents and all children to embrace and take strength from: success and happiness are eminently possible in life with ADD, in many different fields, in many different ways. Not only did the people we profiled achieve professional success, but they were fulfilled and satisfied in their personal lives as well. Each of these people found the good that was buried in what was identified by schools as defective or "bad."

Finding the good in what's bad or identifying what I call the mirror trait is not mere wordplay. It forces you to search for strengths, and in so doing to expand your understanding of ADD from a pathological model to a more accurate, comprehensive model, one that takes into account not just what's wrong but also, more important, what's healthy, talented, and right.

If everyone would include in the definition of ADD the mirror traits, we would be able to understand ADD much more fully and provide assistance much more effectively— not to mention enthusiastically.

Chapter 8

The Cycle of Excellence

A METHOD FOR UNWRAPPING GIFTS

It is one thing to believe it is important to unwrap the gifts embedded in the mind of a child (or adult) who has ADD, but it is quite another to know how to do it. I have suggested you start doing it by embracing a strength-based model and identifying the mirror traits in your child's behavior. Now you need an unwrapping strategy that goes into more detail.

In this chapter I offer an unwrapping plan that I know works, because I have used it myself many times and seen it used many more times. I have spent years developing this plan, a game plan for childhood that any person can use to unwrap his or her gifts, or any parent or teacher can use to unwrap the gifts within any child.

Let me tell a story that shows the five steps in action, then break them down step by step.

Every summer my wife, Sue, our three kids, and I spend the month of August on Lake Doolittle in the tiny town of Norfolk, Connecticut. I have been spending Augusts on Lake Doolittle for some twenty-five years, dating back to before I knew Sue. Our three kids—Lucy, Jack, and Tucker—have spent every August of their lives on Lake Doolittle. Even though there is no TV and the place is so rustic that the only shower is an outdoor shower, our kids love the lake and have always vigorously declined when we've asked if they'd like to go somewhere else for a change.

Each summer I have made it a point to find a new toy we can use on the lake. Some restrictions apply, because the Lake Doolittle authorities do not allow motors on the lake. One way they keep the lake as clean as it is is to forbid gas engines. So one summer I bought a sailboard. Another summer, a kayak. One summer my toy of the year was a trampoline that floats. Another summer it was a huge, inflatable Apollo 15 space capsule.

For the summer of 2007, I brought along the most unusual toy I've ever bought. It was a contraption called an AquaSkipper.

The AquaSkipper looks like a giant yellow grasshopper. It has handlebars and two foot pedals as well as a snout in front that dips into the water and an eight-foot-wide back plane that also dips into the water. Made of light and durable metal tubing and yellow plastic, the AquaSkipper stands about six feet tall and ten feet long.

The object of the game, so to speak, is to stand on the edge of a dock, put the AquaSkipper into the water, grasp the handlebars, put one foot on one of the pedals, and push off from the dock with the other foot. Once both feet are on the pedals, you are supposed to start bouncing up and down, pogo stick style, so that you generate sufficient thrust to keep the AquaSkipper afloat and moving forward.

I had given the AquaSkipper to the family on Christmas morning. However, it had stayed in its box all winter and spring, as there was no place to use it at home. It was meant for Lake Doolittle. Jack—fifteen years old at that time—especially looked forward to trying the AquaSkipper. When I described what it did, his eyes lit up, and I could see how much he looked forward to giving it a try.

When we arrived at Lake Doolittle that year, all of us but Jack made a mad dash into the water for our annual re-baptism. Jack didn't jump right in. Instead, he sat patiently on the dock putting together the AquaSkipper. This was not a simple task, especially because Jack has ADD and hates to read directions. He puts things together by feel—his feel is exceptionally good—but when he comes to an impasse, he experiments before resorting to the directions. When all else fails, he might read the directions, but it pains him deeply to do so.

Within an hour, Jack had successfully assembled the AquaSkipper (it would have taken me a week). Duly impressed, we all gathered around the dock to watch him launch this strange-looking craft. We all imagined, as I'm sure Jack did, too, that he would simply push off and happily bounce his way around the lake.

But no. Jack pushed off . . . and promptly sank like a rock. I then read the instructions. They made it sound so simple. I repeated the instructions to Jack: stand on the balls of your feet, don't lean too far forward or too far backward, push off hard. Jack tried to do that, but once again he sank.

We all finished our swim and went inside to make preparations for our initial use of the grill, another of many rituals to be resumed at Lake Doolittle. In about two hours, after I had the charcoal glowing and the steaks ready to go on, I heard Jack yell from the lake, "Dad, I got it! Come here!" I put down my grilling tools and sprinted the hundred feet or so to the dock, as quickly as a fifty-seven-year-old man with a total hip replacement can sprint.

Jack was standing on the edge of the dock, handle-bars in hand, one foot on one pedal, and one foot on the dock. He said, "Now!" and pushed off. This time when he bounced, the AquaSkipper responded not by sinking but by shooting forward along the surface of the lake. Out Jack went, bouncing in triumph. He circled around and headed back into the dock. As he glided in for a land-ing, the look on his face could have lit up the darkest night. It was the look of a person who has just banked away capital in one of the most important accounts of all in a developing child: the account of confidence and self-esteem.

This story demonstrates the five elements in what I call "the cycle of excellence." The first step is the most impor-tant. It is to create a connected environment for your child. Second is to play. Third is to practice. Fourth is to gain mastery. And fifth is to receive recognition. Recognition connects you to the person or people who are recognizing you, thus completing the cycle, bringing you back to con-nect.

Here is the cycle:

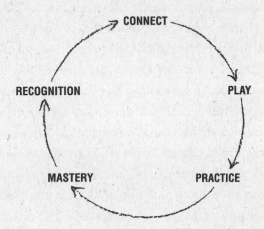

Step 1, to create a connected childhood, is crucial. Many kids these days are growing up disconnected. They may have all the material advantages, but they lack the most important advantage of all: emotional connection to people, places, and activities they love. A connected child feels positively involved in a world larger than himself. He feels—and *feel* is the crucial verb—held in place by loving and caring arms. It is a feeling that precedes words and goes deeper than beliefs or knowledge. This feeling is like an inoculation against despair, a vitamin that propels positive growth. Indeed, I call it the other vitamin C, vitamin connect. As I said at the start of this book, the key to growth and the best development of any child is love. And love begets the feeling of connectedness.

Of course, when I suggest that you create a connected childhood I am not referring to electronic connections. Electronic connections, including cell phones, e-mail, instant messaging, and the Internet, define modern life, including modern childhood, and make it unique, like nothing the world has ever seen before. I embrace that. I am no Luddite harrumphing that we must turn back the clock or at least turn off all our electronic devices, as the airlines like to call them. However, electronic devices, like ice cream or spinach or vitamins or anything else, serve best in moderation. When the electronic connections come to replace all other connections, then they are as dangerous as if ice cream, spinach, or vitamins replaced all other foods. The danger of electronics is that they are so seductive, if not addicting, that unless a parent is careful, a child can become stunted in his or her development due to overuse of electronics.

A robustly connected childhood may indeed, and probably should, include electronics. I say "should" because, correctly used, electronics promote both learning and relationships. However, they are far from defining what I mean by a connected childhood.

A connected childhood includes multiple points of positive connection, multiple points that hold a child in place, stabilizing her and giving her joy as well as direction.

Important points of connection—areas of connection to develop, nurture, and promote—include at least the following:

Connection to family. This is the heart of a connected childhood. But "connected" does not mean "without conflict." The opposite of connection is not conflict. The opposite of connection is indifference. The way to create a connected family is simply to spend time together, talk, interact, discuss, argue, even fight. Just don't disengage. Have dinner as a family. Go on outings together, from trips to walks to the ice cream parlor. Honor traditions, rituals, holidays, and birthdays.

Connection to friends and neighborhood. The glue that holds a life together is often friendship. Encourage your children to make and keep friends. Set an example in your own life by making time for friends and hanging in there with friends, even when it isn't easy. Remember the words of the poet W. B. Yeats: "Think where man's glory most begins and ends and say my glory was I had such friends."

Connection to school or work. The key here is not what grades you get in school or what your pay level is at work, but how comfortable you feel at school or work, how welcome, how safe, how alive.

Connection to activities you love. Encourage your children to try everything they can. Childhood is a time to explore and find out what you like, what you love, and what you can leave aside. The more activities you find that you like, the greater your chances of being happy all your life.

Connection to the past. Cultivate a connection to the past through stories told by grandparents, stories you tell of your own childhood, and stories of your ancestors and family traditions, struggles, triumphs, and hopes.

Connection to nature and special places. Kids naturally connect to nature. Just get them outside. And special places—such as tree houses and swimming holes—are part of the legitimate folklore of childhood.

Connection to the arts. Music, rhyming, dress-up, painting—children are natural artists. By connecting to the arts they can begin to develop a lifelong interest in one or more.

Connection to pets and other animals. All kids ought to have a pet if possible. Pets provide a special connection, like no other.

Connection to information and ideas. The key here is not how much you know or how many ideas you have at your fingertips but how comfortably connected you feel in the domain of information and ideas. The greatest learning disability is fear. Make sure your child does not feel afraid around information and ideas.

Connection to groups, teams, clubs, institutions. Groups such as these instill a sense of responsibility as well as providing an introduction to the power and joy of a group or team effort.

Connection to a spiritual realm or practice. Make sure there is time for some kind of spiritual connection in the life of your child. This does not have to be an organized religion, just some forum for wondering about the ultimate questions. It is good to give kids a place and a forum to do this. They are natural wonderers. Encourage their spiritual wondering.

Connection to yourself. The connection to self develops naturally as these other connections grow. It is magnificent to watch as a child gradually gets comfortable with who he or she is and does not have to put on airs or pretend to be anyone except himself or herself. If you create a richly connected childhood, developing the connections listed above, a positive connection to self will naturally follow.

The great beauty of a connected childhood is that it is available to *everyone*. It is free. There is no test one must take to gain admission to it, no exclusionary criteria, no dress code or pledge required. All you have to do to create a connected life for yourself or your child is determine to do so.

Love and connection go hand in hand. If you create a connected childhood, you will naturally create a loving childhood. This is where parents should spend their greatest efforts, especially with kids who face challenges such as those that ADD can produce.

In the example of Jack and the AquaSkipper, you can see how positively connected he felt at the lake, how easily he could take chances and allow himself to fail at first. He also felt a connection to the tradition of a new water toy each year. Seeing the toy at Christmas gave the kids a chance, in the middle of winter, no less, to connect to a summer tradition. It gave us all a chance to remember and relish that this is who we are, this is what we do as a family.

Such a connection is not about buying the toy or having the money to rent a summer place. It is about creating traditions that support family connection. The tradition can be as simple as watching the ball fall in Times Square on television on New Year's Eve, or going to church on Sunday and having Sunday dinner after that, or tailgating at an annual football game. These traditions can cost nothing but time. But what they give back in connection is priceless.

As it did with Jack, connection leads naturally to step 2 in the cycle of excellence, which is to play. By play, I mean any activity in which a child's imagination gets involved and his mind lights up. You can play making your bed, imagining the sheets to be ghosts or the walls of billowy caverns. You can play solving a geometry problem, as you tinker with one proof after another until the most elegant one pops out. You can even play picking up dog poop in the back yard, as my son Tucker does as he races with our Jack Russell terrier, Ziggy, from one poop to the next, plastic bag in hand. Any activity can be turned into play if the imagination gets involved. In play, children discover the world as well as what kind of mind they have, what they love, and what they want to do more of. In play, they grow. In play, they develop the feeling about life of "I can do it" and "I want to do it," the feeling of looking forward to tomorrow. These are strong predictors of a happy life, far more significant than grades or trophies.

Having connected with the lake and our family, and having connected with the AquaSkipper, Jack began to play with it. He assembled it, which in itself was a form of play, as he used his imagination as his prime guide. Once assembled, the AquaSkipper awaited its first ride. Jack tried and sank.

This led Jack to step 3 in the cycle, practice. Practice that emerges out of enthusiastic play, as it did in this instance, lays down habits of discipline that actually last. Jack kept trying to make the AquaSkipper work. He tried and sank many times before he finally began to get better.

Getting better at an activity that is both challenging and important to you is step 4, which I call mastery. Jack got better at riding the AquaSkipper, so he achieved mastery. By mastery, I don't mean that you become the best at a certain activity. Being the best or being a star are false idols our culture foolishly and dangerously worships. What matters is making progress. If you become the best or become a star in the process, great. But the goal ought not to be a star but simply to do your best with each effort and so make progress. If you do that, your best will get better and better. That's what I mean by achieving mastery. Its effect is magical.

Making progress at an activity that is challenging and important to a person is the single most powerful force we have for building self-esteem and confidence. Self-esteem and confidence are major predictors of success and joy in life, so it is eminently worthwhile to build them. Mastery also is the most powerful motivator we have. Parents often ask me, "How can I motivate my child?" The best answer is simply to set them up to achieve mastery—that is, make progress—at an activity that is both challenging and important to them. People naturally and automatically want to do more of what they're getting better at, especially if it is important to them. There need be no other incentive, bribe, or reward than the great feeling of getting better at an activity that's challenging and important.

But this step, this golden step called mastery, cuts both ways. If, try as you might, you get no better, if, try as you might, you only feel frustration, then that is a confidence buster, a self-esteem breaker, as well as a powerful demotivator.

Therefore, it is imperative for a parent, teacher, coach, or any other person working with a child to set each child up to make progress, regardless of skill level. Skill level is irrelevant. What matters is getting better. Every child can get better at everything, given encouragement and tutelage.

Once you achieve mastery you naturally receive recognition, which is step 5. As Jack mastered riding the AquaSkipper, we all noticed. Family and friends alike congratulated Jack on his progress at this difficult activity. Jack beamed. It was great to see. He grew in all respects.

By recognition, I do not necessarily mean that you win a prize or get the lead role. I simply mean that someone notices your progress. Someone—a teacher, a teammate, a parent, a friend—gives you a pat on the back or a silent nod, some word or gesture that lets you know that that person sees and values the progress you have made. Such recognition solidifies the confidence, self-esteem, and motivation that mastery engendered, while also connecting the child to the person or group who recognized her.

Thus the cycle is complete. Starting with connection, the child ends up connecting. The connection that recognition supplies not only reinforces what mastery laid down but, just as important if not more so, such recognition is a great source of moral behavior. Most bad behavior—stealing, vandalism, lying, cheating, acts of violence—is committed by kids who feel disconnected, kids who feel dissed, disrespected, devalued, disliked, excluded, mistreated, misunderstood, and generally disregarded. An effective program in moral education ought really to be a program in connection.

A connected community spawns far less immoral behavior than a disconnected one.

The single most important treatment for ADD—or for any child, anywhere, at any age—is to enter into this cycle of excellence. The beauty of it is that it's open to everyone, everywhere, always. To enter, all a person has to do is want to.

Parents ought not to worry as much about grades as about their child's progress in this cycle. Make sure your child has a connected childhood. Make sure your child gets the chance to try as many activities as possible; that's how you discover where your brain lights up, where you can most naturally play.

"Once I learned not to fight it, things began to quiet down. Time will not stop and the earth will not end if my son doesn't do his homework."

—Cathy, mother of a son with ADD

"Don't let other people tell you that your child isn't good enough. Schools, teachers, extended family, soccer coaches, churches, and Sunday school teachers may all say this at one time or another. Don't believe them! Just look for other opportunities where your child can succeed!"

—Marlene, mother of a child with ADD

The mistake most parents, teachers, and coaches make is that they jump in at step 3, practice. When problems arise, they ask for more work. They ask the child to try harder.

Trying harder will usually help somewhat, but asking a person to simply try harder is sort of like asking a nearsighted person to squint harder. Eyeglasses work better.

Creating a connected childhood and opening up opportunities to play provide the eyeglasses. A child may get poor grades in school but still be in the cycle of excellence. His future is bright. Another child may get top grades but be leading a disconnected, joyless childhood. His future is not bright.

A strength-based model fits neatly into the cycle of excellence. As you search for talents and strengths, you naturally create opportunities to connect and play. Once you have steps 1 and 2 in place, the cycle runs almost on automatic pilot. Your child starts to look forward to doing something tomorrow. That is all you really need for a child to do well in life.

I urge you to take this cycle seriously and use it in your child's everyday life. It is the best, most reliable way to unwrap your child's gifts while developing the all-important qualities of industry, self-esteem, confidence, desire, enthusiasm, friendliness, and moral rectitude. Not only will your child benefit enormously, but so will you and your whole family.

Chapter 9

Conation

A NEW WAY OF TAPPING INTO
EVERY CHILD'S STRENGTHS

In 1999, my whole family took a trip that led us down the New Jersey Turnpike in the middle of the night. Around 1:00 A.M. we pulled into a motel, booked one room for the five of us, and collapsed into beds, our clothes strewn around the room and on the floor.

At 6:00 A.M., my then-eight-year-old son, Jack, shook my shoulder and said, "Dad, I'm awake."

"I can see that, Jack," I sleepily replied.

"Can I watch TV?" he asked.

"No, Jack," I replied. "We're all still asleep. Why don't *you* go back to sleep, too?" With that, I rolled over and instantly returned to dreamland.

An hour later Jack shook my shoulder once more. "Dad," he eagerly announced, "look what I've made." Knowing that those words might bode ill, I sat up and looked around the room. Rubbing the sleep out of my eyes, I gradually discerned what looked like a thick cord extending from the handle on the door across the room to a handle on the window. As I looked more closely, I could see that this motley cord was made of all our clothes, tied together. "Dad," Jack proudly proclaimed, "it's a clothesline!"

Jack, who has the gift of ADD, was forever doing creative stuff like that. Sometimes what he created was useful, sometimes not, but it was always interesting—and still is. What I didn't understand at that time in the motel room was that Jack had perfectly demonstrated for me his conative strengths. That's because I had no idea what the word *conation* or its adjective, *conative,* meant. What I have learned about those words since has been one of the most exciting intellectual discoveries I've made in the past twenty-five years.

An Important New Idea

I learned about it all from a remarkable woman named Kathy Kolbe. Kathy is the daughter of E. F. Wonderlic, who developed some of the most widely used psychological tests for skills assessment in the business world. Kathy grew up surrounded by stacks of quantitative assessments of various aspects of the mind. With assessment in her blood, she went on to develop her own theory and her own assessments.

At the heart of Kolbe's work is the identification of an individual's natural or conative strengths. Your conative strengths constitute your instinctive way of creative problem solving and making decisions. Your conative strengths are inborn and unchangeable. They have nothing to do with your IQ. They are not good or bad, high or low, strong or weak—any more than hair color or being left- or right-handed is. They also have nothing to do with your emotional makeup or style. They occupy their own, unique realm in the mind, and combine to create what Kathy calls your natural MO, or modus operandi—your natural way of interacting with the world, of solving problems, of initiating actions. You can see the MO in action even in toddlers; it's why one toddler picks up a clock and looks at it while another picks up a clock and throws it, yet another walks past a clock and ignores it, and a fourth stares at a clock and bursts out laughing. Your conative strengths drive what you naturally and spontaneously do, as opposed to what you are told to do or feel you ought to do. People do their best when allowed to use their natural conative strengths. They get frustrated and do poorly when told that they mustn't.

To get a look at a person's conative strengths and his or her MO, give that person a pile of junk and ask her to make something out of the junk. Her conative strengths will dictate what she does next, assuming no one gets in her way. One person will ask endless questions before even looking at the pile of junk. She will get annoyed and even angry if her questions are not answered. Another will dive right into the junk, putting this and that together before the instructions have even been completed. If you ask her to wait while you give more instructions, she will simply tune you out. Another will listen to the instructions, then carefully sort out the pile, separating the overall junk into categories of junk—metal here, cloth there, broken items here, organic matter there. Another will spend considerable time pondering the pile before taking any kind of action. She will put her chin in her palm, cock her head, and stare. You will wonder what she is thinking, but rest assured, she is thinking.

Each of these approaches is "right" for the given person

involved. There is no absolute right way to attack the problem. The different ways *all* have merit. Which you decide to use is not determined by how intelligent you are (whatever that elusive word means) or how you were raised or what your emotional makeup might be. It is determined by a function long overlooked in psychology: *your conative strengths*.

You can think of the mind as composed of three domains. One is emotion, or affect. Another is thought, or cognition. The long-overlooked third is *conation,* the action-oriented part of the mind that leads you, say, to tie clothes together and string them across a motel room between 6:00 and 7:00 A.M. versus all the many other things you could have done during that hour.

All three functions are important. Emotion is the on/off switch. Emotion starts the engine. Emotion generates social style, ambition, and motivation. Emotion triggers conation to take action. Given the pile of junk, you might feel anxious, confused, excited, or even angry at being given such a silly task. Your conative selector decides how you will act, react, and interact with the emotional energy you feel. It will *naturally* select the actions that help you perform at your best—without prior instruction or training. This generates the pattern of your behaviors and a sense of purpose. Cognition or thought then ponder and edit what you are doing, leading to a finished product, whatever that might be.

Four Conative Traits

Having tested more than half a million subjects on her Kolbe A (Adult) Index and Kolbe Y (Youth) Index, Kathy has discerned four major conative traits or Action Modes, as she calls them. Her tests locate you on a scale from 1 to 10 in these four Action Modes. A score of 1 is not bad, nor is a score of 10 good, any more than light green is better than dark green. The numbers simply reflect the pigmentation, so to speak, of a given strength.

The scoring vocabulary in the Kolbe Index runs counter to most tests we take. Usually we expect to get a "good" score or a "bad" one. Here there's no good or bad, but the vocabulary of scoring can be misleading because it is so different from what we usually get in tests. A score of 1 sounds bad because it is a low number. A score of 10 sounds good, as if it were a "perfect" 10. In gymnastics or diving that may be true, but in conative traits it is completely wrong. There is no such thing as an excellent score or a failing grade. The numbers *describe* you, but they do not *rate* you.

Each conative trait ties into a human instinct Kathy has identified. If you score 1, 2, or 3 in a certain trait, you are called *resistant* in that mode. If you score in the middle, 4, 5, or 6, you are called *accommodating* of that mode, which is to say that you can operate that way or not, depending on the situation. And if you score 7, 8, 9, or 10 in a mode, then you are called *insistent* in that mode, which is to say that you insist on acting that way.

Kolbe has named the four conative traits Fact Finder, Follow Thru, Quick Start, and Implementor. Once you understand the Kolbe framework you will be amazed at how beautifully it explains many differences between people, while getting rid of the stigmatizing notion of disability. And what's more, understanding the concept of conative strengths and coming to identify which ones an individual possesses has enormous practical implications for how children learn, how they perform in school, and how to bring out the best in them. Bear with me, as it's worth working to understand this powerful tool. It's probably new to you, so learning about it will take some patience and persistence, but it will be worth it.

Okay, let's dig in. Since you can be resistant, accommodating, or insistent in each mode, and since there are four modes, that means there are twelve conative styles or strengths, as follows:

1. Fact Finder, resistant
2. Fact Finder, accommodating
3. Fact Finder, insistent
4. Follow Thru, resistant
5. Follow Thru, accommodating
6. Follow Thru, insistent
7. Quick Start, resistant
8. Quick Start, accommodating
9. Quick Start, insistent
10. Implementor, resistant
11. Implementor, accommodating
12. Implementor, insistent

Every person must have four of the twelve strengths named above, based on this classification, one in each of the four modes, Fact Finder, Follow Thru, Quick Start, and Implementor. Remember, the "resistant" label connotes a strength just as "accommodating" and "insistent" do.

Once again, it is worth noting that the vocabulary can be misleading. It may sound good to be accommodating and bad to be insistent or resistant, but that is not the case. All three are good, just as chocolate, strawberry, and vanilla are all good flavors of ice cream. You may prefer one over the other, but that does not mean the ones you reject are bad; they're just not to your liking.

We are so accustomed to being rated and graded in life, starting in school and continuing forever, that we reflexively perceive ratings even when they are not intended. So please be clear: your conative style is perfect for you, whatever the numbers are. All scores are perfect scores, just as all shoe sizes are perfect shoe sizes for whichever feet they fit.

Being resistant, accommodating, or insistent in each zone of an Action Mode drives you to act through a *natural strength*. Scoring low in one mode does not mean you are weak in that mode; it means you resist doing things the way people who score high in that mode like to do things. No one mode is better, stronger, or more effective than any other—any more than red hair is better than black hair, mathematical ability is better than artistic talent, or loving baseball is better than loving basketball.

THE "FACT FINDER" TRAIT

An insistent Fact Finder (score of 7–10) has a drive to be *specific* and to gather lots of data before making a plan. This is the person who will ask a thousand questions before doing anything with the pile of junk. He will need to check sources, double-check data, and seek more information when others would stop short. His strength lies in gathering information, and if he is frustrated in doing this, he will not perform at his best.

A resistant Fact Finder (score of 1–3), on the other hand,

has the strength or ability to *simplify* things, and will grow impatient with all this searching after fact and reason. He needs to get on with the show. If he is forced to listen to too many instructions or to recite too many facts, he will get frustrated and not do his best.

An accommodating Fact Finder (score of 4–6) will go either way, depending upon resources and pressures; this is the conative strength to accurately *explain*. Those who can accommodate help the resistant and insistent ones work together.

THE "FOLLOW THRU" TRAIT

A person long on Follow Thru (insistent) has a natural drive to *arrange* and make sure that matters are properly scheduled, that plans turn into actions, that all systems are well coordinated and integrated. An insistent Follow Thru person (score of 7–10) would be the one who arranges the pile of junk into subpiles and sub-subpiles.

A resistant Follow Thru (score of 1–3) is a natural multitasker, and easily *adapts*. This person can change sets quickly, reverse direction, juggle a complicated schedule without losing track of what's going on, and orchestrate the needs of many others without losing focus. He does not need to see one task completed before starting in on another, while the insistent Follow Thru usually does.

The strength of an accommodating Follow Thru is to *maintain order.* He can help the resistant and insistent work together without getting angry with each other.

Interestingly, teachers are usually insistent Follow Thru types, while people with ADD are typically resistant Follow Thru types. If they do not understand the Kolbe framework (and few do), they will attack each other's style as being bad. The insistent Follow Thru teacher will call the resistant Follow Thru student undisciplined, impulsive, irresponsible, unmotivated, too easily distracted or led off task, more interested in stimulation than education, and other variations on the theme of bad. The resistant Follow Thru student will deem the teacher rigid, vindictive, boring, pedantic, uninspiring, stupid, dull, repetitive, and other variations on the theme of bad. Neither the teacher nor the student is right, but they fundamentally misunderstand each other, which leads them to attack each other. The Kolbe framework carries the power to fix all of that.

Before explaining the next two modes, let me just pause to comment on how revolutionary this way of looking at how people naturally solve problems truly is. Almost always, children are taught a right way to solve a problem. Usually, "a" right way becomes "the" right way. If a child is not naturally inclined to do it or can't do it "the" prescribed right way, he is deemed deficient and in need of help, if not punishment.

But in the Kolbe framework, there is no deficiency. Everyone is perfectly capable of creatively solving problems. The key is for them to discover and use the strengths that come naturally to them. Kolbe's is a thoroughly strength-based model.

THE "QUICK START" TRAIT

A person long on Quick Start drives toward innovation, *improvises,* creates risks, thrives on being novel, and avoids what's standard and conventional. People with ADD tend to be long on Quick Start; in Kathy's terminology, they tend to be insistent Quick Start types. The insistent Quick Start will take the pile of junk and start putting together the most unlikely combinations, trying to create the most surprising of all possible junk creations.

On the other hand, the resistant Quick Start might grow angry, even indignant, at being asked to perform a task with so little instruction, guidance, or explanation. Teachers tend to be resistant Quick Start types. Their strength is to *stabilize*.

The accommodating Quick Start, as with all accommodators, can bring peace to the conflict. While the insistent Quick Start is screaming, "I'm bored with all these instructions, let's just jump in and get started!" and the resistant Quick Start is sternly responding, "Now just slow down here and act responsibly for once in your life," the accommodating Quick Start can intervene with, "If we just wait a second or two, then everybody will feel comfortable, and we can all jump in together, so let's hold on and do this as a team." Their strength is to *mediate*.

THE "IMPLEMENTOR" TRAIT

A person long on Implementor needs to use his hands and naturally *builds*, shapes, crafts, and constructs. My son Jack is long on the Implementor function. On the Kolbe Y Index, he scored a 7 in Implementor. That's why, given a room strewn with clothes, he ties them together and fashions a "clothesline," while someone who leads with Follow Thru insistence might have picked up the room and organized everything. (Mothers love insistent Follow Thru types.) While someone like Jack, an insistent Implementor, spontaneously builds and constructs, the resistant Implementor has an ability to *imagine* solutions but isn't likely to physically make it happen. A resistant Implementor is someone like me, a bit of a klutz when it comes to being a handyman at home. I may see that the shower head needs to be changed, but when I try to do it myself, I twist the pipe too hard and break it off. Then I turn to someone like Jack for help! The accommodating Implementor could go either way. He could see that the shower head needed to be replaced, and he has a pretty good chance of being able to do it himself, but he could also ask for help from someone more skilled if that person were available.

Knowing your conative strengths can help you enormously in life. It can guide you in deciding what kind of work to do, and it can help you sort out problems with other people. A huge proportion of conflicts in the workplace, in school, and in relationships derives from an unacknowledged clash of conative drives.

Let's look at school as an example, since this is where many kids with ADD struggle and flounder. In 2006, Arizona State University studied a sample of more than five hundred students and their teachers. They all took the Kolbe Index to assess their MO or conative strengths. What the study found is highly instructive and useful.

The teachers' conative strengths were typically in the higher range in Fact Finder (66 percent) and Follow Thru (62 percent). The conative strengths of students identified as ADD were the opposite: two-thirds of them were naturally resistant to Fact Finder and Follow Thru actions. Their conative strengths were as insistent Quick Starts and Implementors.

The implications of this study are profound and, once you understand Kolbe, obvious. The data show how grossly mismatched most students identified as ADD are with their teachers. While the insistent Fact Finder/Follow Thru teacher expects students to organize, research, and attend to details, the insistent Quick Start/Implementor student, who is often considered to have ADD, needs to experiment, take chances, and solve problems in a hands-on way. This leads to many of the conflicts involving kids with ADD in school settings.

It would be useful for teachers and students to understand such conative conflicts and see them for what they are—a difference in innate strengths—before turning these differences into a power struggle or disciplinary matter.

It is unlikely that teachers around the country will suddenly embrace Kolbe's work and start striving to assess and understand their conative strengths and the full range of conative strengths among their students. It is unlikely that teachers will suddenly understand that many kids identified as having ADD tend to be insistent Quick Starts and Implementors, which puts them naturally at odds with most teachers, who are usually resistant to those types of actions and interactions. It is unlikely that a new approach will suddenly burst upon a nation of teachers (or parents, doctors, or any other group, for that matter).

However, it is *likely* that you who are reading this book do want and can gain such enlightenment and pass it along to your child. Rather than wait for the day when schools finally get it, it makes much more sense for you and your child to take responsibility for managing the teacher, instead of hoping the teacher will learn how to manage your child. Fair or not, this is the way it is. Like it or not, kids who can take control of their education get a *much* better education than those who can't.

> "At the beginning of each year, I spend time with [my son's] teacher, explaining my son's condition and some of the strategies that help him. The teachers know to keep his desk near theirs, to use positive reinforcement, and to give him special jobs to do instead of trying to keep him seated at his desk quietly. He has been in charge of the class library or told to write a book that will be published for the school. It makes him feel important but not different."
>
> —Angela, mother of a child with ADD

What I advise you to do first of all is to take the Kolbe A Index online (www.kolbe.com) so you can get a definition of your own conative strengths, then have your child take the Kolbe Y Index online, so he can get a definition of his conative strengths. Once you both know how these natural drives work, you can then begin to develop strategies for your child in the classroom.

You can also tell your child's teacher about the test and the marvelous ideas behind it. If the teacher is receptive, you—and the teacher—have struck gold, because life will never be the same for that teacher or her or his students. The teacher can take the test and learn from it, just as the students can.

My own Kolbe Index score is 5-3-9-2:

Fact Finder: 5 (accommodating)
Follow Thru: 3 (resistant)
Quick Start: 9 (insistent)
Implementor: 2 (resistant)

You can see that with a 2 in Implementor I come by being a klutz naturally; my strength is in envisioning, not in building. And with a 9 in Quick Start, I am about as insistent as a person can be in that mode, which is often the case for a person who has ADD, as I do. Combined with my resistance to Follow Thru, of course I go nuts when I am told to wait, to listen, to follow directions, to do what I'm told. I practically jump out of my skin. This doesn't mean I am bad, the message kids with ADD get in school, but it does mean I'd better have a plan or risk getting into trouble with various people in authority.

Rather than throw a fit, which is the primitive "strategy" I'd employ if I didn't have better strategies, I have learned to wait simply by drumming my fingers, running my tongue around my mouth, anticipating a great meal, or recalling a great football game. Such seemingly trivial ways of passing the time give me an outlet for my frustration. If the waiting goes on longer, I have a little puzzle game that I play. All I need is a piece of paper and a pencil, and I can draw up the puzzle. It is an initials game. I randomly write down a column of five letters and across from it write down five more random letters, thus creating five pairs of initials. The game is then to think of a famous person with each pair of initials.

It can amuse me through the most boring of waits, the most boring of speeches, the most boring of explanations.

On the other hand, the 5 score indicates that I can accommodate in Fact Finder. While my Quick Start drives me to jump in immediately, whatever the project might be, my Fact Finder acts as a buffer. For example, in writing this book, it was important that I do research first, *before* writing. As absurd as it might sound, my natural inclination is to write the book first. But my Fact Finder protects me from doing that and creating what might be a very bad book indeed. My Fact Finder edits, or puts on the brakes, so I accommodate and do my research. Of course, my MO turns the research into an active adventure, so it becomes interesting in itself. I travel to meet people. I seek out unusual facts and novel treatments for ADD. I discover new ideas and new experts—for example, the new idea of conative strengths and the expert I newly discovered, Kathy Kolbe, for this book. I ask direct and provocative questions. I do what it takes to make fact-finding interesting to me, and use my Follow Thru strength of multitasking to keep it from being rote and dull.

This is the kind of strategizing I urge you to do with your child, especially in regard to school. Once you know your child's conative strengths, you need to help her adapt to the MO of her teacher. It's a safe bet that the teacher is long on Fact Finder and Follow Thru—and certainly the education system itself is that way. So let's say your child wants to do a project in a novel way, as most kids with ADD do. You should coach your child to raise his hand and, when called on, say, "I have researched this problem and I have a solid plan for how to do it." Whatever your child says next is all but guaranteed to be met with the teacher's approval, because people who are long on Fact Finder and Follow Thru believe that research and planning are next to godliness. You child could say, "I have researched the problem, I have a solid plan for how to do it, and I would like to change the sex of the principal," and the teacher might reply, "Good idea. I've been hoping someone would tackle that problem."

I'm joking, of course, but only to make a serious point. If your child can learn to adapt to the conative strength of the teacher, your child will do better in the class. You might hope that the teacher would learn to do that for your child, but hope is not a strategy, and you and your child do need a strategy that works so that school will not become a slough of toil and frustration.

Let's say your child has a Kolbe result of 5-5-2-8: 5 in Fact Finder, 5 in Follow Thru, 2 in Quick Start, and 8 in Implementor. She is therefore short on Quick Start and long on Implementor. She needs stability, and accommodates plans and systems. Being short on Quick Start (the third number) means she is easily upset by anything new. It can overwhelm her. So you need to coach her on asking for help, asking for directions, asking for a system. Most teachers *love* to provide directions, systems, and structure, and they will love your daughter for asking for that. It will allow them to do what they are best at, which will help both them and your daughter. But you must coach your daughter to take the initiative. You can role-play the situation at home.

On the other hand, your daughter has an 8 in Implementor. She is an insistent Implementor. She needs to use a hands-on approach whenever possible. Words likely come hard for her. She will need some coaching from you in basic communication skills, such as making eye contact, listening, and speaking up when spoken to, not mumbling. She is a doer, not a talker, so don't expect her to be chatty. Don't barrage her with questions or pester her for long descriptions of how her day went. She won't naturally provide you with that, and it will only frustrate both of you if you keep drilling her as if she should be able to. She will withdraw even more and begin to lose confidence and a positive sense of who she is if you (and others) keep behaving as if her natural way were bad or defective.

Her gift for the two of you to unwrap will lie in construction, putting things together, crafting, building, and in general acting upon the physical world. Encourage her to do that as much as possible, and also encourage her to let her teacher know that this is how she learns best. The more she can explain herself to her teacher, the better. Make sure she doesn't demand anything from the teacher or seek to get out of any work—deep within most teachers beats a heart that believes that hard work conquers all, and if your child even gives off the faintest odor of a slacker, woe unto her! But you can coach her on how to explain her need to use a hands-on approach when possible. Most teachers actually know of such systems, and your child can open the door for the teacher to use the manipulatables she has stored in the closet.

To offer another example, let's say your child's Kolbe index is 6-8-1-5: 6 in Fact Finder, 8 in Follow Thru, 1 in Quick Start, and 5 in Implementor. I once met a fourteen-year-old boy, whom I'll call Ryan, with that score. He had been diagnosed with obsessive-compulsive disorder, anxiety, and attention deficit disorder.

Setting aside the diagnoses, all of which emphasize pathology, I could use the Kolbe framework to coach Ryan and his parents on how to bring out Ryan's strengths and avoid the pain he so often suffered in school and elsewhere.

Being an insistent Follow Thru, Ryan was superb at developing systems and plans. Being resistant in Quick Start, Ryan also hated sudden change or surprises. You can see how neatly the two could fit together if they were approached as strengths in their own right, rather than weaknesses or disorders. You could urge Ryan to take advantage of his natural way of solving problems to help him with his fear of change and surprise. He could use his ability to make plans and devise systems to help him deal with uncertainty and change. He could learn simple probabilities. He could make Venn diagrams (overlapping circles) of what was certain and uncertain, expected and unexpected, obvious and hidden. Then he could make plans for how to deal with the unexpected and how to ferret out what was hidden. He could use his insistent Follow Thru to help create the structure and stability he so craved. Just having a plan would allow him to feel less vulnerable and more in control, which would instantly reduce his anxiety. All of this would not only help him emotionally but also be useful educationally and give him strategies he could employ for the rest of his life.

Regardless of what Kolbe score your child might have, you can work with your child to come up with strategies and tricks to make learning in school more productive. If she is short in Fact Finder, she can use her strength of seeing the big picture to write down bullet points about what goes on in class. Don't worry about taking copious notes—she'll never use them anyway. If she is long in Follow Thru, encourage her to use that strength to devise systems and plans for getting all her work done and for dealing with the unexpected. If she is short in Implementor but long in Quick Start, coach her to ask for help in the lab part of her chemistry class, and encourage her to offer help in what she's good at, which is coming up with new ideas and dealing with surprises.

Asking for help and giving it in return is a life skill of enormous value. If you can learn it in school, you are way ahead of the game. The goal for your child should not be to become independent. No one is independent. The goal should be to become *effectively interdependent,* to learn how to ask for the help he needs and to be able to offer what he has to give in return. That's life in a nutshell. School is a good place to learn it.

The Kolbe model is one innovative way by which you can introduce your child to her strengths while giving her practical tips on how to take advantage of them. As you and she gain awareness of her MO, you and she will be equipped to brainstorm and develop a system of being effectively interdependent at school—and everywhere else.

Chapter 10

The Kolbe Model in Action

"I'm desperate," a mother told Kathy Kolbe after hearing Kolbe speak. "My wonderful, fun-loving nine-year-old son Andy has become frustrated in school and has developed such low self-esteem that he says he hates himself. I'm really scared because he's tried hard, and nothing makes life better for him. Please help!"

This story was all too familiar to Kolbe. A highly verbal kid who needed to get up and move around was now in a school where speaking up spontaneously and doing anything other than sitting still and listening or writing was considered inappropriate. Her hunch was that Andy's MO (the Kolbe profile, as previously described) would be similar to that of thousands of other kids diagnosed with ADD. They often have conative or natural strengths that don't fit the behavior requirements in standard third- through eighth-grade classrooms.

"What does Andy do well?" Kolbe asked his mother.

"It's almost hard to remember," she said, "because his

teachers give us long lists of everything he does wrong. He's so angry and inhibited now that it seems he won't even try to do anything."

"When you think of him as a little kid, what makes you smile?" Kolbe asked.

"He was silly, and fun to talk with, and had a great vocabulary and inquisitive mind. He was inventive in the way he played, and very good at building things—only to crash into them, of course."

"He sounds like a terrific kid whose natural inclinations may be at odds with those of most teachers and the teaching methods used in most American schools. If my hunch is right, there are some things I can help him do—very quickly—that will make his life much easier and far more fun."

To validate her hunches, Kolbe suggested that Andy complete the Kolbe Y Index. He found it fun to take online, and afterward he read and listened to the audio advice with his parents. They were amazed at how it captured the child they knew, with lots of very positive examples of how he could use his particular natural strengths. His mother told Kolbe: "I can't believe it! So much of what the schools have told us are bad things about Andy the Kolbe Index describes as wonderful strengths. It's as if you've opened a dark curtain and let the light in. We see the hope, but he's been so convinced that there is something very wrong with him that he's having trouble believing he's okay."

"I'll give him a few more suggestions, what I call Conables Tricks, because they'll help him self-manage his conative strengths in very simple, engaging ways," Kolbe said.

Andy's profile was:

3 in Fact Finder, which helps him simplify
2 in Follow Thru, which means he's adaptive
8 in Quick Start, which is why he's so good at
    improvising stories
7 in Implementor, which explains his need to move
    around and build things with his hands

His individualized result also explained how his Fact Finder made him a "once-over-lightly" kid. He didn't get bogged down in too much looking around for information before he was ready to act. His Follow Thru score is the reason he gets bored doing repetitious homework and loses the homework teachers hovered over him to get done. That Quick Start energy causes him to break in when others are talking to add his two cents' worth. His Implementor strength is behind his having trouble sitting still in class.

"I get it," his dad told Kolbe. "Andy's natural strengths are the types that go unrewarded at his school. They may even cause conflicts with some teachers. I guess we've been a part of the problem, too. We've told him to sit still and be quiet. Are you telling us he actually needs to be up moving around while doing his homework?"

"Yes. Don't you know people at work who walk around while they talk on the phone, who create better standing at a drafting table, or who come up with new product ideas while they're brainstorming with others—interrupting and using models to help them visualize possibilities? That's how Andy is likely to make his mark on the world."

Kolbe knows the business world well, having run an award-winning entrepreneurial business she founded thirty-two years ago, been a consultant to Fortune 500 CEOs, lectured at major business summits, and designed management software used around the world. She's heard thousands of stories from high achievers, from Olympic and professional athletes to scientists, artists, and leading educators—many of whom describe their classroom behaviors as being similar to Andy's, and who realize they fit the description of people who are now often called ADD.

"What makes people tick is a constant in their lives," Kolbe says. "What changes is what works in different environments. Andy's conative strengths would make him a terrific pioneer in fields such as product development, sales of tangible goods, fields of science such as physics and geology, playmaker roles in professional sports, and a variety of outdoors endeavors that require dealing with endurance and uncertainties, just to name a few future possibilities."

When Andy heard this list of ways he could excel, his belief in himself soared. "You mean I really could be good at those things, even though I'm having trouble in school?"

"Yes, absolutely." Kolbe hadn't simply guessed at the examples she gave. After twenty-five years of longitudinal research, she knows which MOs are successful in particular types of career paths.

"Many of the top people in those careers tell me stories just like yours," Kolbe assured him, "and they all used tricks like the ones I'll teach you. They're what got them through the times when they needed lots of self-control to keep the energy inside them from causing problems."

"So we need to keep telling him how terrific his conative strengths are," his mom said.

"Not with the ever-present 'Good job!' kind of fluff," Kolbe cautioned. "He does have a challenge, because he was not created to take action the way most schools require kids to act, interact, and react. We find that most elementary-grade teachers have MOs that are almost opposite from Andy's conative methods. Most teachers are long in Follow Thru and need activities to be done in a particular sequence. That type of environment is a problem for Andy.

"I tell kids that their Kolbe result shows that they are perfectly capable of solving their own problems and of making good decisions," Kolbe went on. "But they are responsible for taking control of their abilities and putting them to good use."

Andy, Kolbe explained, needed to rediscover the joy of accomplishment that he had as a young child. He also needed to take responsibility for his own use of this drive, learn to self-manage his strengths, and discover appropriate ways to ask for what he needs.

"You'll discover that you're perfectly capable of doing things the way you need to do them, without disrupting others," Kolbe told Andy. "That's what I've watched professional athletes and others with your abilities learn to do."

Kolbe tailored Conables Tricks to Andy's interests and specific age and skills. After finding out that he really hated writing, dreamed of being a rock star, and loved technology, Kolbe made some suggestions.

"Get used to writing, because rock stars have to sign lots of autographs!" she said. "And use your technology know-how to print out many photos of yourself on which you can write notes of the type you might send to your fans."

These activities engaged his Quick Start and Implementor strengths, as did her suggestion that he produce a brochure of the future in which he would write about his fame and glory. They brainstormed about the use of free online software to design and produce it, or the option of simplifying it by cutting and pasting a Word document over an existing brochure.

The goal was for Andy to figure out how he could best accomplish his own goals. A kid with more Follow Thru might have jumped at the idea of putting the brochure in a scrapbook he'd create to fill (sequentially) with accomplishments, but Andy wisely opted to put it on the refrigerator door. That kept him from getting into a project he probably would not complete. He laughed with Kolbe about how silly it would be for him to even think about opting for lots of steps he'd probably not finish.

"Now, be sure, Andy, that you do this while you're watching TV or listening to music, so you don't get bored," Kolbe added.

"Really? You're saying I *should* do that?" More laughter, of course.

"Why don't you negotiate with your parents to study with music on, and see if you can get your homework done faster and do better that way? If you can, you might see what happens if you study with the TV on. That often makes writing less painful for me. I'm dyslexic, dysgraphic, and I have ADD, yet I majored in journalism. We can all find constructive ways to do what we want to do. I'll bet you could learn very quickly by studying outdoors, even while sitting in a tree. Keeping the wind from taking your papers can be a good way to stay focused on them!"

"Wow, do you think my parents would let me do that?"

"Try asking politely, and be sure to let them know that you will find ways that help you accomplish what you need to do in the time you have to do it. Be prepared to prove it by getting better grades."

A couple of weeks later, Kolbe got an e-mail from Andy's mother:

It's been great fun for the whole family to watch Andy trying out new ways of doing his homework. It seems that just making the physical act of writing more comfortable for him has eased up on his anxiety about written work. We had no idea how much movement is essential for him. No wonder school had become like a prison. Now that we know his conative strengths, and we've completed our own Kolbe A Indexes, we catch ourselves when we start to tell him how he has to do something. Instead we're following your advice and concentrating on the goal and letting him figure out his own way of accomplishing it. We're doing the same thing for all of our kids. What a difference it's made in our family life!

Conables Tricks also helped Andy deal with teachers. Kolbe always suggests that kids try to figure out their teachers' conative strengths. Does Andy see a teacher having conative needs that are similar to or different from his needs? How could he respectfully request that he do something a different way? What changes can he make in how he does things that won't bother his teacher or other students?

Kolbe finds that kids love to come up with their own ideas for making their lives easier and their grades higher. She emphasizes that they need to give themselves constant reminders to find ways to get the right answer or complete the assignment so they can enjoy a sense of accomplishment.

Another of Kolbe's imperatives is that teachers ought not to have to change the way they teach in order to satisfy kids' conative needs.

"I assure teachers that my work will not make more work for them," she says. Andy's teachers never realized that Kolbe had coached this wanna-be rock-and-roll star to watch them very closely. For Andy, the purpose is to focus his attention on imagined bandleaders whom he depends upon to keep him on the right beat and in sync with the other students. She's encouraged him to sometimes pretend that classmates are his all-important backup musicians.

A year after Andy began using Kolbe's Conables, he, like so many other kids who have used the Kolbe wisdom, had become a master at managing his own strengths. His awareness of his conative abilities—and of the differences between those and the ways others need to take action—had made him more of a team player. He was more sensitive to his impact on others, and more likely to seek help from those who offered appropriate strengths when his weren't the best fit.

"Kathy," he said a couple of years after they first spoke, "I think that when I get a girlfriend, I need one who keeps a list of what we are going to do and when we are going to do it. My Follow Thru may be good for multitasking, but I'd sure like to have her keep track of our plans." He was applying what he had learned about himself to all the important areas of his life.

Not every youngster can be in private or small group sessions with Kolbe, so through her nonprofit Center for Conative Abilities, she developed a program that is delivered in schools and through community agencies. She calls this unique, low-cost approach Project: Go Ahead. It's designed with a similar process to the one she used with Andy, providing all kids (with special focus on those diagnosed with ADD) the opportunity to discover their conative strengths and ways to self-manage those innate abilities for success in schools and other endeavors.

"We prequalify schools and organizations for this program," Kolbe says, "based upon their willingness to listen to what kids say they need. There must be evidence of mutual respect between the adults and the kids, just as our workplace programs require respect among leaders and workers at all levels."

A school with both economic and racial diversity brought Kolbe-trained experts in to provide Project: Go Ahead sessions for students. Groups of students with similar Kolbe Y Index results were told: "Your Kolbe results show that you all are perfectly capable of solving problems in a very similar way."

An economically disadvantaged minority youngster, with perilously low self-esteem, looked at the boy from the gifted class who was sitting next to her.

"Wow," she said, "I can hardly believe it. My natural abilities are just as good as yours. That's cool!"

Without her teachers having to do a thing, that youngster began what has become a consistent effort to use her conative strengths to solve her own problems.

"No one ever thought she would be the high achiever she has become," her principal noted. "It's marvelous to watch kids discover how much better they can do when they trust their conative strengths."

Chapter 11

What Should You Tell the School?

As I mentioned in discussing Kathy Kolbe's concept of conation, it is often helpful if you can find a way to get your child's teacher(s) on the same page with you. As I also mentioned, the bulk of the work will need to be done by your child and you, but many teachers and schools are quite open to learning along with you, if you present what you have to say respectfully and concisely.

The question of how to do this comes up all the time. Your child has been diagnosed with ADD and you wonder what, if anything, you should tell the school.

Our advice is to be open and honest—but only after you have developed a trusting relationship with the teacher. The best results *always* come in situations where there is trust and respect on both sides.

Too often, when a child has ADD the parents and the teacher get into a struggle, and pretty soon the school administration joins the battle. No one wins, and the child loses big-time. So beware of the temptation to become adversarial, even if you know you're right and the school is wrong.

Instead, begin by reaching out to your child's teacher. Take the time to get to know your child's teacher a bit before you delve into problems and solutions. Make small talk. Small talk is big. It can be awkward, tedious, even arduous, but it is time well spent. Small talk sets the table for big talk. So ask about the weather, the local teams, the new gym, the old faculty lounge, the new style of clothes the kids are wearing, the ubiquity of cell phones, and anything else that crosses your mind. Then ask about the teacher. Who is she? How long has he been a teacher? Where did she grow up? Does he have kids of his own? What is her philosophy of education? What does he think are the biggest obstacles kids and parents face these days? What would she really like to tell parents if she could just get them to listen? Teachers are experts. It works wonders to treat them as such.

Then ask how you can be of help to the teacher. Do photocopying? Bake cookies? Offer expert advice you might happen to have on finance, health, or other topics of value? Rare is the parent who wants some special treatment for his child who begins by offering special treatment for the teacher.

Of course, you don't have to do that. Technically, the tuition or the taxes you pay ought to cover whatever additional service you need from the teacher for your child. But think about it. Think in your own life how much more likely you are to go the extra mile for someone who has gone out of their way to go the extra mile for you. It's just human nature. The parent who comes on strong with a list of entitlements may get his requests met—but they will not be met as enthusiastically or as effectively as if he first offered to do something extra himself.

Time spent building a positive relationship with your child's school—mostly with the teacher or teachers—is a precious gift to your child. Over the years I have seen hundreds of examples in which the failure to spend that time cost children dearly. And I have seen *many* examples in which spending that time made the difference between a bad year in school and an outstanding one.

It doesn't help to say that life in school shouldn't be this way. It doesn't help to say that, as a parent, you shouldn't have to work at getting your child the treatment he deserves anyway. It is simply a fact that your child will do better in school and like school more if you put in the time to build a positive relationship with the teacher or teachers.

A second lesson I have learned is that the bureaucracy that surrounds "special education" is just that, a bureaucracy. If you can possibly avoid its clutches, do so. Sometimes the services schools offer in their special programs are outstanding. But sometimes they amount to nothing more than glorified babysitting. If you determine that your child's special education classes aren't productive, you'd be much better off hiring a private tutor or coach if you can possibly afford it.

If you can devise an *informal* individual education plan (IEP) with the teacher, do it. That will save both you and the teacher hours of paperwork and contentious committee meetings. Sometimes you need to go the route of the formal IEP and enter into the bureaucratic world from which these plans emerge, but I urge you to try the informal, let's-do-this-on-our-own approach if you can.

How to do that? Just schedule a meeting with the teacher (after you have made the good relationship already mentioned) and ask the teacher what she thinks your child needs. Explain to the teacher that your son, say, has ADD. Ask for her advice on how best to handle kids who have ADD. Perhaps she has experience with kids with ADD. Did she have a child in her class last year with a similar issue? It is always best to treat teachers with the respect that they deserve as experts. You will also get better results if you do this. Really listen to what the teacher says, trying to set aside your agenda and keep an open mind. Doing this makes it most likely that the teacher will do the same for you. Next, offer your suggestions as to what you think your child needs. Then see if the two of you can come up with a plan that makes sense to you both, independent of the special education bureaucracy. Introducing the Kolbe test results I mentioned in the last chapter is a good way to broach the subject of learning and behavioral differences. It can be enormously helpful to teachers to look at these results—nothing speaks louder than this kind of concrete evidence.

If the teacher is open to reading something about ADD, you might offer to show her the following section of this book. I have written it explicitly for teachers. You could show her the whole book, but most people, including teachers, don't have time to read entire books on top of all their other work simply on the recommendation of a parent. However, she might take the time to read these paragraphs, which I have intentionally kept brief.

A BRIEF SUMMARY OF HELPING KIDS WITH ADD, WRITTEN FOR TEACHERS

As the person who gave you this book may have already told you, I have been treating kids with ADD for more than twenty-five years. I also have ADD myself. I hope that my experience can be of some help to you in your efforts to teach kids with ADD.

I endorse and recommend a strength-based model for talking about and helping kids with ADD. This book is all about understanding and using a strength-based model, but if you don't have time to read it, I hope this short section will give you an overview good enough to help you begin to use it in your classroom.

A strength-based model describes ADD not as a disorder but as a trait. I describe ADD to kids as like having a Ferrari race car for a brain with just ordinary brakes. The brakes aren't powerful enough to control the brain all the time.

With that in mind, I urge you to try to understand that the mistakes kids with ADD make are not intentional. Telling a child who has ADD to try harder is about as helpful as telling someone who is nearsighted to squint harder. Their problems with focus, organization, time management, impulsive behavior, and the like are not due to lack of effort. They are due to the biological makeup of their brains. ADD is a heritable trait, highly influenced by genes.

The genes that cause the problems also cause the positives so often seen in kids who have ADD, positives such as creativity, high energy, intuition, sensitivity, bigheartedness, charisma, imagination, curiosity, stick-to-it-iveness when the task at hand really interests them, and the ability to think outside the box.

It is crucial that teachers not lead these kids to think of themselves as disabled, disordered, or "less than." It is crucial that teachers get fear out of the classroom and make it safe for these kids—and all kids—to make mistakes.

As a teacher, you have enormous power to shape a life forever. Let me tell you how my first-grade teacher forever changed my life. Her name was Mrs. Eldredge. When I started first grade in 1955, it quickly became clear that I was not learning to read. Back then, if you couldn't learn to read, your "diagnosis" was that you were stupid, and your "treatment" was to try harder. But Mrs. Eldredge knew there was more to it than that. She had no formal training in reading except that she'd been teaching first grade for her whole career.

During reading period we would all be sitting at little round tables, taking turns reading out loud. When my turn came, I couldn't do it. I would stammer and stutter.

At that moment, Mrs. Eldredge would simply come over, sit down next to me, and put her arm around me. Even though I stammered and stuttered, none of the other kids would laugh at me because I had the equivalent of the Mafia sitting next to me. Mrs. Eldredge's presence protected me from ridicule; her patience steeled me for the task at hand.

That was my IEP: Mrs. Eldredge's arm. It changed my life forever, because it dispelled fear and shame. I never felt ashamed that I was the worst reader in the class, and I never felt afraid of trying to learn. Her arm has stayed around me all my life. I'm still a very slow reader, but I majored in English at Harvard College, graduated with high honors, and now make my living reading, writing, and speaking. That would not have happened were it not for Mrs. Eldredge. Such is the power teachers have.

Beyond stressing strengths and dispelling fear and shame, there are specific helpful steps that you can take in the classroom with children who have ADD. They include:

- Have the kids with ADD sit toward the front of the room (though not all together). Even better, have a circular seating arrangement. That way, someone is always looking at each student. It is very hard not to pay attention when someone is looking at you.
- Use touch if it is allowed in your school. I shudder to think that Mrs. Eldredge's arm is now illegal in many schools in this country. But if you are allowed to, touching a child on the shoulder, say, is a great way to provide encouragement and also bring his mind back into the room and the task at hand.
- Use eye contact. Your eyes can bring attention back into the room.
- Use kids' names. When you hear your name it is almost impossible not to pay attention.
- Never keep kids in for recess. Exercise is essential for mental focus.
- Consider starting the day with some stretching exercises.
- Consider having the kids sit not in chairs but on exercise balls. That provides constant musculoskeletal stimulation, which is good for the brain, and also involves the cerebellum, which is good for focus.
- Emphasize proper brain care with the kids: eat right, get exercise, get enough sleep, don't overdose on electronics.
- Introduce new topics in terms of old topics already mastered. Kids with ADD overheat easily. They get frustrated

quickly when they sense they won't understand something new. So, for example, when you start fractions explain right away that fractions are simply division written differently, and the kids have already learned division.

• Break down large topics or tasks into small, manageable bits. For example, a book report might be subdivided into eight steps, or a science project outlined in a dozen doable steps. Once again, this helps the child with ADD not feel overwhelmed. It is also helpful for all the other kids.

• Notice and appreciate successful moments. Kids with ADD often go through an entire day getting multiple reprimands or therapies without one single affirmation. Imagine how you'd feel if you went through your day like that.

• Stay in touch with parents, even if you don't particularly love them. My best advice to teachers is the same advice I give to parents: make friends with each other.

• Don't let the child or the parent use ADD as an excuse. ADD is not an excuse to get out of taking responsibility but an explanation that leads to taking responsibility more effectively.

• Don't fall into the trap of the "moral diagnosis," blaming the child's difficulties on bad character. Look deeper than that. ADD is a neurological trait, not a moral infirmity.

• Above all else, enjoy these kids. Nothing works better than that—for both the kids and for you.

Chapter 12

Schools That Get It Right

The day I met Marjorie VanVleet I told her that she was from heaven. She modestly dismissed the remark, but she is. She saves the lives of children the world has turned its back on.

Imagine running a school whose main admission requirement is that the students have failed at all other schools. Imagine running a school where most of the kids have ADD or some other learning difference, and you have no budget for special education services. Imagine running a school where you are your own support staff, and your entire faculty numbers four, including you. Imagine running a school of forty students between the ages of sixteen and twenty-one, 60 percent of whom come from families who live below the national poverty level and many of whom have a history of violence or crime.

Welcome to the Corning–Painted Post High School Learning Center (HSLC) at Corning Community College in Corning, New York. Welcome to the world of Marjorie VanVleet and her school, which offers living proof that if you run things right, kids can unwrap the gifts in their minds, no matter who they are or where they're from.

This is not an elite school as traditionally described because poverty is one of the admissions requirements. It is a fully accredited school that takes students the mainstream schools have rejected or found impossible to educate. It has precious few resources other than the imagination and devotion of the faculty. There are no traditional demarcations between grades—freshman, sophomore, and so on—but rather a world of learning and work open to all. Necessity was the mother of Marjorie VanVleet's invention, but it is an invention we all can learn from, as this school *could* be set up anywhere. Operated on an ultralow budget, the school takes any low-income child who wants to attend and who has been unable to learn in mainstream settings. A teacher's nightmare? No, Marjorie VanVleet's dream come true.

Marjorie loves her school and her students. In its fifth year of existence, the HSLC has a 93 percent daily attendance rate. The kids love the school. They all work at paid jobs around town in the morning, and then they have three hours of class in the afternoon. Again, not the traditional schedule for a school, but one that leads to excellent results.

Classes are imaginative. Although Marjorie VanVleet was not familiar with Kathy Kolbe and conation when we first met, the teaching at the HSLC allows each student to use his or her natural conative strengths. For example, to learn math the kids might go rock climbing and develop the Pythagorean theorem against the wall of a rock face. If a student doesn't like a book he is supposed to read, he is allowed to pick another book. "There are so many books, after all," Marjorie explained to me. "I just want these kids to read. I don't care all that much what they read, just as long as they read."

The school teaches English, history, math, science, and foreign languages, but in nontraditional ways. For example, in science the class made biodiesel fuel and then learned how to purify it and use it to run an engine. Another science class constructed a functioning hovercraft.

Lest you believe this is all loosey-goosey, alternative education that does not prepare students for the real world, the pass rate from the HSLC on the New York State Regents Exam last year was 76 percent. That surpasses the pass rate of many mainstream New York high schools. One might say that since the class size is small the kids have an advantage, but they don't have traditional classes at all—kids learn by working on their own, having discussions with each other, and meeting with teachers one-on-one, as well as meeting in groups that could be called classes. But that small "advantage" is more than offset by what most people would see as all but insurmountable disadvantages: few teachers, low budget, no special education programs, and a school full of kids with special education needs, who have failed already.

Since all the students at the HSLC had failed in mainstream public schools and most of them came classified as ADD or otherwise learning disabled, one might wonder how the HSLC does meet their special needs. One of the first things the HSLC does is "declassify" the students, which removes them from the special education system altogether. Many experts would maintain that this dooms them to repeated failure, but, miracle of miracles, once removed from the special education system, they do better. That's because VanVleet embraces a strength-based model.

The "system" with which Marjorie and her staff replace regular special education combines—without their having known about either model—the five-step method I have outlined earlier with the Kolbe conative-strength model, thus proving that people can arrive at the same solutions without having necessarily read the same books or subscribed to the same beliefs.

What Kathy Kolbe, Marjorie VanVleet, and I do have in common, however, is the fixed belief that all students have gifts and that those gifts can be unwrapped only if the people in charge create the conditions that allow for each person to learn and live in the way he or she is *naturally inclined to do.*

Not every kid who applies to the HSLC gets in. Not only must they have failed at other schools, but they must also write an essay explaining why they want to attend the HSLC. A committee then interviews them. This committee is composed of the merchants who will employ them in the morning hours, the faculty of the school, and some other students.

Once a student is accepted, what opens up to them is a kind of schooling entirely different from anything they have experienced before. *Learning* becomes inevitable, no matter what a student's style might be.

There are three rules at the school. First, no drugs or alcohol are allowed at school or at work. Marjorie says she can't control what goes on at home, but she encourages the students to be moderate if they drink, and most comply.

The second rule: no violence, either physical or verbal.

In five years, there has not been one fight at the HSLC. How many New York public schools can match that?

The third rule: no plagiarism. The students insisted on that rule, as they had heard what a problem plagiarism was at other schools. Originally, Marjorie had forgotten to include no plagiarism in her set of rules, but the students alerted her to the problems that that omission could create.

In addition, the school espouses certain guiding principles. The cornerstone principle is respect. The others are responsibility, excellence, ethics, leadership, and growth. Every ten weeks the students do a self-assessment of their personal growth, their academic growth, and their service to the community. They then present this to a panel in the format of, "I once was _____, now I am _____." For example, a student might report, "Ten weeks ago I couldn't calculate the area of a triangle or circle, I couldn't converse intelligently with a customer at the hardware store on which paint to buy, I couldn't honestly state that I was sober every day, I had not manned a kettle for the Salvation Army, and I hadn't read *Huckleberry Finn*. Now I've done all that or can do all that. And ten weeks ago I couldn't have written this in complete sentences."

The kids are extremely proud of their achievements, and rightly so. After all, these are the kids most of the world had given up on when they arrived at the school. They knew they had something positive to offer, but most adults had deemed them impossible to teach. At the HSLC, they get a chance to prove those people wrong. As one said, "I'm glad people have found out we're not throwaway kids." Far from being throwaways, 60 percent go on to college. All but one who have graduated are now either in college or employed.

But what the school instills goes way beyond these impressive statistics. The school engenders in each student feelings of confidence, hope, enthusiasm, and pride not only in who they are but in the community they are a part of. The kids graduate eager not just to advance their own lives and careers but also to help others do the same.

There are many other excellent schools around the country that use a strength-based model, such as the Landmark School, north of Boston and the Carroll School near Boston; the Rye Neck Public School System, in Rye Neck, New York; the Lamplighter School and the Shelton School, in Texas; and the Curry Ingram Academy near Nashville, Tennessee. I have written about these schools in other books. I'd like to mention two additional schools here.

The first is the Leelanau School, near Traverse City, Michigan. A boarding high school, Leelanau accepts boys and girls from around the country who have ADD and other learning differences.

I have spent time at Leelanau and have seen firsthand how beautifully and brilliantly the school works to bring out the best in each student. Located on the shore of a lovely lake, the school actually has one classroom located practically on the beach. The English teacher who runs that classroom is one of those geniuses who can make books and ideas become riveting for absolutely anyone. When I visited his class, I didn't want the period to ever end—and neither did the students.

The head of the school, Rich Odell, is a pioneer. He has brought together a faculty composed of men and women who love the adventure of teaching people who naturally think outside the box, and maybe need help even finding the box. These teachers love the students—and what a difference that makes! Typically, students arrive at Leelanau short on hope and long on lethargy. But within weeks that changes. They get excited because for the first time in a long while, their teachers are excited about them, and other kids are interested in them. What develops is a cauldron of connection, a crucible of enthusiasm for life, full of laughter, learning, and the "long, long thoughts," as Longfellow called them, that ought to populate a young person's mind.

Without knowing it, Leelanau uses Kolbe's ideas as well as my ideas embedded in the five-step cycle described earlier. The school focuses on finding students' strengths and giving them methods of compensating for shortcomings.

I was so impressed with Leelanau that I now run a summer camp program there with Rich Odell. We run weeklong sessions for students who have ADD *as well as their parents.* Each morning one of the gifted teachers from Leelanau meets with the kids for three hours. They learn about ADD and how to study, but in such a fun way that they love it. They learn from each other as well as the teacher. Above all, they learn that they have major gifts, not just weaknesses, and that they can expect to do extremely well in life. In just a week, they get a big helping of knowledge, skills, hope, confidence, and joy. One girl, who originally had not wanted to attend, asked her mother at the end of the camp, "Mom, can we come back to ADD camp next summer?"

While a teacher meets with the kids, I meet with the parents. Imagine thirty parents gathered in one room, all of whom have at least one child who has ADD, and many of whom have ADD themselves. It makes for a dynamic week.

Each morning, for three hours, I teach the parents what I know about ADD. But, even more importantly, they teach each other what they know. They share stories. They cry and laugh together. They get angry together, and they plan new ways of dealing with people who just don't get it. As the week progresses, anxiety and fear diminish as hope, excitement, and positive energy rise. By Friday, the final day, they are all offering tearful goodbyes as well as vowing to stay in touch. They all head home with fresh ideas and renewed determination to make sure their children unwrap their gifts.

The camps have worked so well that Rich Odell and I are expanding them to include more summer sessions. To learn more, just go to the Leelanau website, leelanau.org.

The other school I want to mention briefly is the Purnell School in Pottersville, New Jersey. Founded in 1963, Purnell is a boarding high school for girls who have had trouble in other schools or who learn differently.

As at Leelanau, when students get to Purnell, everything changes. They find their strengths, they gain confidence, they succeed. The 125 girls who attend this school soon fill with excitement and find a zest for life that will sustain them forever.

Part of what makes Purnell so special is the head of the school, Jenifer Fox. Jenifer has worked in education for years to develop a curriculum specifically designed to identify and promote strengths. "Many schools want to do this," Jenifer told me, "but they don't have the methods or the systems developed to be able to do it regularly and consistently with all students. What we've developed here at Purnell is a curriculum, a method, that works with everybody."

Fox has put this method into a brilliant book called *Your Child's Strengths*. If you combine what's in that book with what's in this book, including the Kolbe profile of conative strengths, you will have a guaranteed means of identifying and developing your child's strengths.

I know of no book that offers as practical and useful a curriculum for developing strengths as that in *Your Child's Strengths*. While Purnell specializes in learning differences, Fox's methods can be used in any school by any teacher. She gives the specifics, the exact how-tos, that teachers and parents need. To learn more, you can go to the Purnell website, purnell.org, or the website devoted to the book, yourchildsstrengths.com.

What if you don't have access to one of these magical schools? No matter. My purpose in describing the schools was not simply to praise them but also to show you how you can begin to change the school your child attends as well as the childhood you offer your child.

By creating a connected childhood, by emphasizing strengths, by supporting family traditions, by working with your school to eschew humiliation as a teaching tool and instead to embrace a no-fear policy in the classroom, by finding the right tutor or the right summer camp, by making time for hanging out and doing nothing, by resisting the modern tendency to turn childhood into a frenzied and pressure-packed preadulthood, by insisting that childhood ought to be a protected time for play and exploration, growth and development, you can turn any childhood into an ideal childhood, even without access to an ideal school.

Chapter 13

Making a Diagnosis and Composing a Treatment Plan, Including New, Alternative Approaches

As we mentioned in the introduction, this book does not present the details of diagnosis and treatment that our other books do. In this chapter we offer a brief overview of how to make the diagnosis of ADD and what can go into a treatment plan. I also describe some new approaches to treatment that, while not yet proven in double-blind studies to be effective, I believe are promising. Given our different backgrounds, with my twenty-five years' experience seeing many patients and Peter Jensen's twenty-five years in rigorous scientific research, he and I have different thresholds for embracing treatments that have not yet been scientifically proven. But that's okay. Clinical experience is where hunches open our eyes to new discoveries, and science is where our clinical hunches get formally tested. That's also why we began our collaboration in this book.

The Resources section at the back of this book will give you suggestions for books and other materials that provide greater detail about diagnosis of and treatment for ADD. One helpful website worth mentioning here as well, however, is one that I've had a hand in creating. This site will connect you to others who are interested in the same issues, and it will also allow you to get help with actual diagnostic issues and treatment plans. The company I am working with takes its name from the skilled individuals who help others climb mountains such as Everest; it is called Edsherpa (edsherpa.com), as in Sherpas devoted to education. It is not up and running yet, but should be some time in 2009.

The following sections provide a summary of what you ought to do.

Diagnosing ADD

There is no one test for ADD. As with all the diagnoses we make in psychiatry, this diagnosis is based primarily upon your child's history. The story of the child's life should reveal ADD if it's present. Therefore, the best "test" for ADD is the oldest test in medicine: the patient's own story.

People often get confused about this. Even doctors do. We can't tell you how many people have come to see us for a second opinion having been tested for ADD and found not to have it. Their doctors had believed that a neuropsychological test or a brain scan could rule in or rule out the diagnosis of ADD. So the patients first received some test, which, when negative, put an end to the diagnostic process then and there.

Big mistake! To diagnose ADD, you should not start with tests; you should start by taking a careful history. The history must come from the child, the parents, and the child's teachers. Children with ADD are usually not very good self-observers, and parents are also not particularly objective in observing their own children, so teacher reports become a vital part of the history.

I prefer to get narrative comments from teachers rather than checklists. Peter likes to do both. Even though the checklists, such as the Connors checklist, have been standardized and validated, they miss much. They lead the witness, so to speak. I would much rather simply ask a teacher to write a few sentences about Johnny or Marie. This gives the teacher the chance to say whatever comes to mind, and will include more valuable information than a checklist ever could. If the diagnosis truly is ADD, the symptoms will often appear in the teacher comments if the child's difficulties aren't complicated by other problems that worry the teacher more, such as difficulties reading, or severe oppositional behavior.

However, you may have to read between the lines to see the symptoms. I have read so many teacher comments that I can quickly tell what is going on. Often what I have called elsewhere in this book the "moral diagnosis" creeps in and camouflages the symptoms of ADD.

For example, if a child has trouble paying attention and getting organized—classic symptoms of ADD—the teacher comments might read like this:

> Chris must learn to discipline himself and pay better attention. He must not let himself get distracted

so easily. He must make the effort to work hard, even when he is not interested. He must remember to bring all his materials to class and to be on time. He must not get so sidetracked in conversations. He must not speak out of turn. He is selling himself short because he has much more talent than his grades reflect. It is especially distressing because sometimes he performs at such a high level, only to tail off into poor performance an hour later. It all comes down to commitment and hard work. I hope he resolves next semester to give us his best.

I have read hundreds if not thousands of comments like that one. You can see embedded in the morally tinged rhetoric the textbook symptoms of ADD: distractibility, trouble getting organized, inconsistent performance, underachievement, and impulsivity. The mistake this teacher makes is the most common mistake that many teachers make with regard to ADD: *the teacher ascribes all of the student's problems to lack of effort.* The teacher doesn't understand that the problem is not one of effort but one of brain wiring.

In reviewing the history as elicited from the parents, child, and teachers, an experienced clinician can make the diagnosis of ADD. He can supplement his diagnosis through neuropsychological testing, which is always interesting but never definitive of the diagnosis. Many kids who have ADD are able to focus during neuropsychological testing because it is so highly structured, being done one-on-one, and full of novelty—puzzles and games and conundrums. Neuropsych testing is fun! The child is usually also motivated to beat the test, which adds to the mental focus. So, it is not uncommon to get false negatives on testing.

That does not mean you shouldn't get the testing done. It can be helpful, particularly if other conditions are contributing to the child's problems, such as a learning disability. Neuropsychological and formal educational testing often provide a wealth of information that the history alone cannot provide. In addition, they are often required by schools if a child is to get accommodations. So consider getting testing if there is any question about what is going on; just don't hang your hat on it to make the diagnosis.

As mentioned earlier, I urge you to have your child take the Kolbe Youth Index by going to kolbe.com. It is great if parents take it as well, so they can see how their styles match up. Most people who do testing will not have heard of the Kolbe test, so you will need to explain it to them, just as you will need to explain it to the teachers. But if you can do that, you will be helping the teacher and your child enormously.

The question of where to go to get a diagnosis often comes up. Many disciplines train people in ADD. Child psychiatrists get the most training, but we are in short supply. If you can't find a child psychiatrist, you might consult a developmental pediatrician, a child psychologist, a pediatric neurologist, a social worker who has had special training, or any other clinician who has learned about ADD and has experience. For example, some family practitioners are superb at this.

The best thing to do is to get a referral from someone who has had a good experience with a given clinician. Look around. We have seen hundreds of children who have wasted years because they did not see a clinician who truly understood ADD. Such unfortunate waste can be prevented if you simply look around and keep looking until you find someone who you know in your gut is skilled and a good match for you and your child. We have found that other parents will often be your best source for guidance about who's really good in your community for diagnosing and helping kids with ADD and figuring out when something else is going on.

Treating ADD

This book has explained a strength-based approach, and that should be at the heart of every treatment plan. You ought to look at treatment as the unwrapping of gifts, not as the rectification of a disorder or the filling in of a deficit.

Every treatment plan should include:

1. Diagnosis, including the identification of talents, strengths, interests, and dreams
2. A Kolbe assessment with subsequent action steps based upon the Kolbe strengths profile
3. Implementation of the five-step plan I call the cycle of excellence
4. Education of the family and the school as to what ADD is and is not
5. Changes in lifestyle
6. Structure
7. Counseling of some kind
8. A consideration of medication
9. A consideration of various other therapies

STEPS 1–4: DIAGNOSIS, KOLBE ASSESSMENT, CYCLE OF EXCELLENCE, EDUCATION

See chapters 4, 5, 8, 9, and 10 for information on whom to consult for a diagnosis, the Kolbe model, the five-step model, examples of using a strength-based approach, and how to deal with the school.

STEP 5: CHANGES IN LIFESTYLE

The five major areas to focus on here include:

• *Sleep.* Most kids with ADD don't get enough sleep. Enough sleep is the amount of sleep that it takes for a person to wake up without an alarm clock. If you don't get enough sleep, you'll look like you have ADD whether you have it or not.

• *Diet.* Eat a balanced diet of whole foods. Try to avoid junk food, sugar, additives, and dyes. Just don't have them in the house. A recent study published in the prestigious medical journal *Lancet* showed that additives do indeed increase hyperactivity, so stick with whole foods. I recommend that you give your child omega-3 fatty acid supplementation in the form of fish oil every day, while Peter Jensen is less certain of the need for this. The brands that I know are reliable are OmegaBrite (omegabrite.com) and Dr. Barry Sears's brand, Zone Labs (zoneliving.com).

• *Exercise.* Daily physical exercise is essential for optimal brain function. My friend and colleague Dr. John Ratey details the copious research that drives this point home in his groundbreaking book *Spark: The Revolutionary New Science of Exercise and the Brain.* All children ought to exercise every day. Never deny a child sports. Never keep kids in from recess. Make sure your child does not become a couch potato or video game potato. Not getting exercise is as bad for the brain as getting exercise is good for it.

• *Prayer or meditation.* We now have abundant evidence that meditation, prayer, or other mindfulness exercises promote mental focus, emotional balance, and physical health. Pioneers such as Herbert Benson at Harvard and Jon Kabat-Zinn at the University of Massachusetts have proven beyond any doubt that these practices promote all forms of well-being. Sue Smalley at UCLA has shown how helpful these practices are in working with ADD. Kids can easily learn how to meditate, pray, or perform other mindfulness exercises.

• *Positive human contact.* We include this in the list of essential lifestyle changes even though most people do not think of it as a lifestyle issue. But indeed it is. It may be the most important item on this list. As I've said, I call it the other vitamin C, vitamin connect. Positive human contact—a friendly hello, a pat on the back, a good laugh with a friend—is a potent tonic for the mind and the body. Not getting enough positive human contact—which is the case for many children who have ADD—causes a deficiency syndrome just as surely as not getting enough ascorbic acid (the traditional vitamin C) does. Make sure your child gets some kind of positive interaction with other people several times a day. It is easy to forget this when you become preoccupied with all the therapies and remediations.

STEP 6: STRUCTURE
Structure refers to any external device that you set up to compensate for what's missing internally in the mind of

someone who has ADD. For example, kids with ADD do not have as many filing cabinets in their brains as they need. So you need to set up an external system to help them keep track of what is due when. The best system is the one you create with your child, specifically designed to meet his or her organizational needs. One size does not fit all.

Structure is a small word but a huge tool. Properly used, structure can control many of the negative symptoms of ADD. The main reason students with ADD have such a hard time the first year of college is that they lose the structure their parents provided at home when they go away to college.

People with ADD often resist structure because they think it is boring, uncreative, and tedious. Their real reasons, though, are that they find it painful and alien. But it is essential.

You must work with your child to make friends with structure. It can feel like making friends with a porcupine: one touch and you're in pain. But persist. Find the right alarm clock (my son who has ADD has an alarm clock that flies around his room; to turn it off he *has* to get out of bed). Find the right filing system. Find the right way to remember to bring home all your books (an alarm in the book bag that goes off at the time the student leaves school is one idea). Find the right study schedule (often short spurts of study with many short breaks work better than long, uninterrupted hauls). Find the right study setting (one of my patients did her best work sitting on the kitchen floor, her back leaning against the dishwasher while it was running). Make sure you schedule in time for exercise.

Sometimes a book on getting organized can help. There

are many. One good one is *Getting Things Done* by David Allen. Above all, approach structure with a creative spirit. Understand that structure can really set you and your child free. Far from holding you back, structure allows you to get the most out of your talents.

STEP 7: COUNSELING

Often a person who plays the role of coach can help a great deal in setting up the organizational systems these children need. It can be difficult for parents to do this because what I call the "nag factor" gets in the way, and the process becomes a power struggle. But when you hire an organizational coach to work with your child, the nag factor disappears, and the process can flow more freely. ADD coaches are becoming easier and easier to find, but you want to be sure you find a good one and one who is a good match for your child. Nancy Ratey is a master coach, and she has written an excellent book on the topic called *The Disorganized Mind*. That book also has information on how and where to find the right coach for your child (or for yourself).

Various kinds of psychotherapy can be useful. Behavior therapy—the systematic use of rewards and consequences to assist the child in learning to control the impulsivity and hyperactivity that is causing problems for the child (and you)—is the most-tested, best-proven form of counseling. But remember, without the child buying into it and without a good relationship with the child, as Peter Jensen's experience with his own son illustrates, behavior therapy can backfire. Often in families where there is ADD a recurring pattern develops that I call the "big struggle." Every day, everyone squabbles with everyone else. Just getting done what needs to get done—homework, dishes, bath, and the like—becomes hugely difficult, because everyone is digging in, objecting, refusing, accusing, ignoring, yelling, blaming, stomping, and in general making no progress. A few sessions with a skilled behavior therapist can work wonders in breaking up the big struggle. Family therapy focused on these issues can also be helpful. You have to be a wise shopper here, however, because some family therapists might mistakenly assume that the problem is because "Mom is too lax," "Dad travels too much," or "the marriage needs fixing" when the core issue might be the child's ADD.

STEP 8: CONSIDERING MEDICATION

Medication is by the far the most-researched and most-proven intervention we have for ADD. Stimulant medications—such as Ritalin, Adderall, Concerta, and Dexedrine—have been used to treat what we now call ADD since 1937. No medication remains in use that long—more than seventy years—unless it is both safe and effective in the great majority of instances. Most people fear medication because they do not know the medical facts. The truth is that when stimulant medication is used properly under skilled medical supervision it is as safe as, if not safer than, aspirin.

But most people have a negative gut reaction when the idea of medicating their kids comes up. We urge you to try to get emotion out of the way and look at the facts. When people ask us if we "believe in medication," we tell them that medication is not a religious principle. It is a matter not of belief but of scientific fact: when used properly, the right stimulant medication is 80 to 90 percent effective in helping people who have ADD to focus more clearly. The other 10 to 20 percent get no benefit or can't tolerate the side effects. Used properly, there should be few or no side effects other than appetite suppression without unwanted weight loss.

If you find a doctor who is skilled at regulating and adjusting these medications, you stand a very good chance of getting benefit from a stimulant medication. The benefit can be as powerful as eyeglasses are for nearsightedness. Suddenly the child can focus. Suddenly performance improves. Strengths emerge. Confidence and motivation grow. A positive upward cycle replaces the downward one.

When people balk at the side effects of the stimulants, we first tell them that these are easily eliminated as long as the medication is prescribed properly. Side effects may include appetite suppression, insomnia, agitation, blunting of personality, elevated heart rate, elevated blood pressure, headaches, nausea, and tics or involuntary muscle movements. All of these side effects are immediately reversible by lowering the dose of the medication or discontinuing it altogether. We believe that a child or adult need *never* suffer long-term side effects as long as the individual receives proper medical supervision. After we explain to the parents the possible side effects and how they can be handled safely, we then ask them to reflect upon the side effects of *not* giving the medication: years of frustration, underachievement, and self-doubt.

Medication is not a cure, and it should never be the only treatment. But when used as part of a comprehensive, strength-based plan, it can be phenomenally helpful and safe.

STEP 9: CONSIDERING OTHER THERAPIES

Most of this book has been about one nonmedication therapy, namely, the concerted and organized effort to develop strengths and talents as well as emotional balance and joy.

But what else is there? In fact, quite a number of alternative or complementary treatments are gaining in importance. Let me discuss the three that I am most familiar with and currently use in my own practice.

Fish Oil

The first is the use of fish oil as a dietary supplement that provides omega-3 fatty acids. I discussed that earlier.

Cerebellar Stimulation

Peter Jensen and I agree that we need more research here and that so far this treatment is not *proven* to be worthwhile. However, we both agree that it is promising. The cerebellum, a large clump of neurons located at the back of the brain, has long been neglected because people did not understand how involved it is in higher brain function. It was thought that it simply controlled balance, coordination, and automaticity, the "automatic pilot" of the brain. But now, thanks to the work of Jeremy Schmahmann at Harvard and others, we know that the cerebellum sends connections to the front of the brain, and exerts a much more powerful influence on the thinking part of the brain than we ever knew.

Various innovative clinicians have believed this for years, and have based treatments for ADD, dyslexia, dyspraxia, and other conditions on a regimen of physical exercises that stimulate the cerebellum, even though scientific research has not yet established the efficacy of this. Programs such as Brain Gym and Learning Breakthrough offer what I feel are promising programs, as do specialists in occupational therapy.

One program that both Peter and I are familiar with that uses cerebellar stimulation is the program developed by Wynford Dore and his team in England. I first learned about it in 2003 because my son Jack had a problem. Jack was able to read, but he *hated* doing it, and trying to get him to read led to bitter struggles. None of the standard tutoring interventions helped. It was an awful problem, one that I, a specialist in the field, was unable to fix.

Then I heard about Dore. I met the man, as well as Roy Rutherford, his chief researcher, and learned about the exercises that stimulate the cerebellum. Dore explained to me that if Jack would do these simple exercises for ten minutes twice a day for a period of months, maybe a year or so, there was a good chance that it would fix his resistance-to-reading problem.

The exercises were simple—standing on a wobble board, standing on one leg with eyes closed, juggling, and the like—but they did have to be done faithfully, twice a day, every day. Knowing that just getting Jack to brush his teeth could take some doing, I wondered if this could work. But then my wife, Sue, volunteered to do the exercises with Jack. Sue always had a problem with driving over curbs and getting lots of flat tires every year, and Dore explained to her that these exercises could help her with that problem, so she and Jack embarked on a journey together. Every day they'd stand in the kitchen in the morning and in the evening and do the exercises.

For a few months there was little if any change. But then, about four months into the program, something amazing happened: Jack started to like to read. I couldn't believe it. I was grateful beyond words, and excited as well. I set about learning all I could about the method.

Now, four years later, Sue has not driven over any curbs since she started the exercises. She and Jack both did them for about eight months, then stopped. Their improvement has been permanent.

I used to be a paid consultant for Dore, so you might say I am biased. However, I was paid only to offer suggestions, not to hype the method. One of the services I provided was to introduce Peter Jensen to the Dore method.

Peter is a world-class researcher. Given the lack of scientific studies of the role of the cerebellum in ADD, he got interested. He found independent funding and has embarked on a prospective, carefully controlled study, comparing the Dore method to a control group and to medication. The study won't be complete for a few years, but it will give us the data we need to endorse this program more emphatically—or not.

For various reasons the Dore company has had difficulty sustaining itself commercially. As of this writing, the company has closed down, but hopes to reopen in the future. We continue to offer the cerebellar stimulation treatment at my offices in New York City and Sudbury, Massachusetts. The future of the Dore operation may be in doubt, but the future of cerebellar stimulation as a treatment remains an exciting area of active investigation.

Beyond Dore, other clinicians have tapped into the power of cerebellar stimulation. You can learn about two of the best on the Web at Learningbreakthrough.com or Braingyhm.com.

In the meantime, my experience tells me that the Dore method may be a reasonable alternative treatment. It may help; it may not. The Achilles' heel of the program, in my opinion, is compliance. It is not easy to get a child to do ten minutes of exercises twice a day for months on end, especially if there's no immediate benefit. For the program to work, you need to do it with someone, as Jack did, or make sure there is a coach or some other supportive person involved. And even with Jack, it did not replace the benefit he receives from carefully managed medication.

Neurofeedback

Here Peter and I agree that this treatment is not yet formally proven effective. For years neurofeedback, a therapy that provides real-time information about brain wave activity and helps teach people to change those patterns of activity, had made sense to me, but I didn't use it in my practice because it seemed too cumbersome and expensive. In traditional neurofeedback, the client has to go to the practitioner's office once or twice a week for thirty or forty weeks, each session costing around $100. For a therapy that was unproven, that seemed like too much. Still, the basic idea continued to appeal to me.

Then, several years ago, I gave a presentation at a conference where I met Dr. Len Ochs. He told me about a new form of neurofeedback that he had developed. In his version, the client typically only needs fifteen to twenty sessions, and each session involves only a few minutes of brain stimulation. There is no hour-long active training, in which the client works, for example, to make a car go faster across a screen; instead the client sits passively for a few minutes as ultra-low-energy radio waves, one-thousandth of the energy you get from a cell phone, are passed through the brain. As treatments continue, the brain-wave readings change.

Ochs calls his method low-energy neurofeedback stimulation, or LENS. He has had good results with it in treating a variety of conditions including ADD and anxiety. Ochs doesn't know exactly how LENS works, but it has helped many people with ADD and anxiety.

I was so impressed that I asked one of the clinicians who works with me, Rebecca Shafir, to get trained in LENS. Not only did she get the training, she now offers LENS as an alternative treatment for clients who come to my center in Massachusetts, and we also offer it in my New York office. We have seen excellent results, especially in adults who have ADD. LENS seems to help them come out of their fog, without medication.

The more I learned and the more positive results I saw, the more impressed I became. I wondered what LENS would do for me if I had the treatment. My ADD is under control; I have unwrapped my gift, so to speak. But I'd had one symptom for most of my life that bothered me: I couldn't stop worrying about stupid stuff. It made me less happy and calm than I should have been. So I thought I would try LENS and see what happened.

It was amazing. My friends, my wife, and the people who work with me will all tell you that I am more relaxed and less reactive than I've ever been. I can tell you that a black knot inside me has been untied. I don't brood and ruminate the way I used to. And no, I am not on the payroll of LENS. I am just a very satisfied customer!

Without Peter's prompting, let me hasten to add that this is purely anecdotal evidence and means nothing scientifically. Just as with cerebellar stimulation, we need carefully designed, prospective, controlled studies by independent researchers. But it seems to me foolish not to report on what I've seen and experienced just because a study has not yet been done.

There are various other alternative, complementary treatments that people have found beneficial, from acupuncture to chiropractic to an assortment of nutritional interventions. I always tell my patients that I am willing to explore any treatment with them, as long as it is safe and legal. By being open to what's new, we learn.

On the other hand, it is a mistake not to take advantage of what we know works: a comprehensive, strength-based approach that includes all the elements laid out in this chapter.

Chapter 14

A Collaboration Convened—Please Join!

With this book, a powerful collaboration is convened that could change millions of lives. The collaboration is not just between Peter Jensen and me, but between us and the thousands of people we have treated and consulted with during our combined fifty-five years of practice; between us and the many others in the strength-based movement, including school heads Jenifer Fox, Marjorie VanVleet, and Rich Odell as well as researchers such as Martin Seligman and George Vaillant; between us and the hundreds of other colleagues who have helped us with their research and wisdom; between us and the tens of millions of people who we have not met who care about children; between us and teachers and students everywhere; and between us and the echoes of the past, traditions we learn from even as we try to change them, practices that teach us even as we strive to reshape them. With this book, we want to invite *you* into this collaboration; we hope you in turn will invite others. It is time for things to change. The only way for that to happen is for us all to join in and make it happen.

Throughout the book, we hope you felt a growing sense of accompaniment and connection, a conviction that not only are Peter and I with you, but that millions of others are with you, too: parents of kids who have ADD, parents of kids who don't know what their kids have, and the kids themselves who are searching and struggling to go where they could, if only they could find the right way.

Years ago, Priscilla Vail, a great pioneer in the field of learning, called such kids "conundrum kids," because no one knew exactly what was going on with them except that they were smart kids with school problems. That phrase became the title of her book, which is now a classic: *Smart Kids with School Problems*. Priscilla has since passed away, but her ideas live on stronger and more sparkling than ever. She stands bright and beautiful in this grand collaboration.

She is one star among many through the centuries who always *knew* there was more to the story than smart versus stupid, normal versus abnormal, bright versus dull, quick versus slow. This collaboration draws upon all those who have known that these kids have special talents and gifts, people who devoted their lives to trying to figure out how to unwrap those gifts. We also draw upon all those children and adults who worked so hard, as Priscilla used to say, not to find the easy way out but to find the *right way in*.

Thanks to her and many others, more children and adults are now finding the right way in than ever before in history. Not all of us experts agree on what that right way in might be, but we all agree that we want what's best for you and that we're on your side—on the side of parents and their children who are trying their best to bring out their best, and on the side of adults who are trying to unwrap their gifts even now. You are all courageous people, and we are proud to work with you.

We hope you feel the warming presence now of legions of teachers, doctors, and other professionals who *do* care and who *do* get it, even if there are some who still don't, and we hope you feel a growing confidence in sticking up for yourself and your child; in knowing where to look for help; in knowing that, far from being alone, you are in the midst of an effort that is welcoming more people every day, an effort that will change the face of education and of daily life for these wonderful but often challenging boys, girls, men, and women.

We hope as you join this proud collaboration, whose numbers grow every day, that you feel ownership of this undertaking. You. Me. Us. That's the way, the only way, we will carry the day.

You are an expert in your own right. You know important bits of information and strategy that no one else knows. We all need *your* help—your ideas, your time and your energy. We want *you* to feel the hope *we* feel, not just the frustration; we want you to feel the conviction we feel that there is a better way and that the better way will prevail sooner rather than later in the life of your child and every child, even when it seems unlikely that this will ever happen.

So much in life these days is contentious and polarizing; this effort should not be. Our first goal has been to extend a helping hand in this book. We want to build bridges and help others do the same. A curse of modern life is that it can be terribly isolating. When ADD is thrown into the equation, it can be doubly or triply isolating. The worst of life happens in isolation.

You need feel isolated no longer. A huge community stands eager to welcome you and help you, knowing that you will help us as well. Parents and families who have been there, and their youngsters who not only survived but even thrived, show all of us the way for more success experiences. Organizations such as Children and Adults with Attention Deficit/Hyperactivity Disorder (CHADD), the Attention Deficit Disorder Association (ADDA), the National Alliance on Mental Illness (NAMI), and others are in fact alliances of parents, consumers, youth, and health care professionals. These and other organizations listed in the back of this book are our best partners in this process, and they offer the latest scientific information, support, encouragement, and models of success. We also offer an overview of the diagnosis and treatment of ADD, and many places to get help.

So as you close this book, take heart. Look up from where you are with a smile and a cheer: a smile born of knowledge that gives you power and sets you free, a cheer born of seeing frustration come to an end, a smile born of determination and the conviction that you—we—will prevail, a cheer born of seeing a child's or adult's best efforts pay off more than you ever dared hope.

You can join us in this collaboration by visiting my website, drhallowell.com and signing up for my mailing list.

Talk to your friends. Start a support group of your own or join the local chapter of CHADD (chadd.org). The more people you involve in this collaboration, the more powerful we all become.

Join us. Together we will create the kind of world these kids—and adults—deserve, a world in which each person can unwrap the gifts he or she was born with, a world in which no child grows up afraid and ashamed of how his or her brain works, a world in which every child can conceive a dream and then pursue it, stoutheartedly, confidently, with every reason to expect success.

Acknowledgments

Peter and I join in thanking the many parents and children who so generously offered their stories, advice, experience, and wisdom to help create this book. They are the best teachers. They are the bravest researchers. They are the warmest collaborators. They are the truth-tellers, par excellence. We are forever in their debt.

We also thank the many scientists and clinicians who have broken new ground in developing both the science as well as the clinical lore that underpins our treatment of ADD. Once a myth or a fad, ADD is now a well-recognized syndrome thanks to the innovative and persistent work of our esteemed colleagues. They are too numerous to name, but, as the saying goes, they know who they are. We thank you all for making it possible for us to write this book, and more important, for millions of children to get help, children who were all but lost only a generation ago.

We would also like to thank the great team at Ballantine Books, led my our superb editor, Marnie Cochran, as well as Jill Kneerim, agent, teammate, and friend.

EDWARD HALLOWELL

I would also like to thank my friend, colleague, and some-time collaborator, John Ratey, for his advice and encouragement through the years. When he was my chief resident at the Massachusetts Mental Health Center in 1978, he stressed to me the primary importance of the human connection, which was to become the most important lesson I ever learned in my entire career. While it is important to be smart in psychiatry, John helped me embrace the far more important qualities of being able to connect with and of being kind to all people in all states of mind, of being receptive to all that is new and different, and of caring more about people than advancing one's own point of view.

I also thank my dear friends, Peter Metz and Michael Thompson, for giving me their abiding love and support for the past three decades. Their friendship and kindness have kept me upbeat, even when I felt down. I have been lucky to make other glorious friends along the way, wonderful people like Ellen D'Ambrosia, Tom Bliss, Jon Galassi, Susan Galassi, Alex Packer, Ken Duckworth, Alan Brown, Paul and Christine Sorgi, Thor Bergersen, Pat and Ben Heller, Gillian Walker, Eric and Sarah Myers, and Joe Polish. I name these friends, not only because I love them, but because connection is the central message of this book, and they have taught me so much about connecting.

I also want to thank my partner in the book, Peter Jensen. Peter's involvement in this book instantly doubled its impact because of his impeccable scientific and academic credentials, as well as his unusual candor in sharing his own personal experience. Peter did what many people never do: he took a chance for the sake of others. Even though Peter is a Mormon, I think of him as a mensch.

Of course, my cousin-who-is-really-my-brother, Jamie Hallowell, has been teaching me about love and connection since I was born. Along with his sister, Josselyn Bliss, who died too young, the three of us used the connection we felt with each other to negotiate the sometimes troublesome waters of a New England WASP childhood. Jamie, Josselyn, and I turned to one another and found not only safety, but adventures, mischief, and joy. From them I learned before I knew what I was learning that all you really have to have is one or two reliable friends and you'll be just fine.

Then Josselyn married Tom Bliss and a whole new world of connectedness opened up, one child at a time, a world that thrives today, years after Josselyn's untimely death at the age of fifty-six.

I also thank my actual brothers, Ben and John. We were not all that close growing up because they were so much older than I, but we are close now. Ben and John are unique. Each is remarkable in his own way. Each has taught me a lot, and I love them both.

Finally, I thank the people to whom I dedicated this book: my wife since 1988, Sue; my daughter, Lucy; my son, Jack; and my son, Tucker. The joy and excitement I feel with the four of them surpasses anything I ever could have imagined. The other day Tucker, age thirteen, saw a saying on a paperweight that read, "What would you attempt to do if you knew you could not fail?" He asked me, "Dad, what would your answer to that be?" I replied, "Exactly what I'm doing." To which Tucker replied, "Right answer, Dad." Kids are the best.

But there would be no kids, and no me, without Sue. I can never thank her enough. But I can try!

PETER JENSEN

Like Ned, I salute the parents of children with ADHD, particularly those from CHADD (Children and Adults with Attention Deficit/Hyperactivity Disorder), who shared their most important "life's lessons learned" about their experiences as parents of children with ADHD. I am equally indebted to parents of children with other conditions, such as autism and autism spectrum disorders, anxiety disorder, depression, bipolar disorder, and schizophrenia—all of these parents have been my wisest instructors of all I know about child psychiatry. Along with them, my other finest instructors have been my own children—all five of them—Rebekah, David, Jonathan, Lisa, and Ben, including two with ADHD. While I sometimes like to jest "they got it from their mother," any one who knows both me and Suzy, knows better. And from Suzy I learned many of my own life's important lessons, most particularly patience with one's own children, a hard lesson for a father who also has a good dose of ADHD. I want to thank my mother, Amy H. Jensen, from whom I learned to believe that I might someday become a doctor, and even to hope that I someday might write books for others! I thank my dearest friend and intellectual companion, Kimberly Hoagwood, whose keen intellect and clear vision inspires in me a continued commitment to serve children and families. And last, I thank Ned Hallowell, a remarkable physician-psychiatrist and human being who has courageously dared to speak out and write positively about ADHD, fueling the essential fires of hope in parents, children, and families, even as we scientists sometime inadvertently dampen the flames by focusing too much on ADHD's negative aspects. Thank you, Ned, for allowing me to add my voice to yours, and to this critical message of hope and healing.

Appendix A

USING BEHAVIORAL STRATEGIES

Strategies to Help Your Child Improve His or Her Behavior
FOCUS ON THE POSITIVE
- List at least three good things about your child. Your child has wonderful qualities and strengths; it is important to remind yourself of these.
- List at least three good things about how you parent your child.
- Post these lists on your refrigerator.
- Celebrate them!

TRY TO REDIRECT (NOT STOP) TROUBLESOME BEHAVIORS
- Children with ADHD are energetic, are spontaneous, and they have a short attention span (there's so much to do!). Reminders in a neutral tone, such as "Remember, we're getting ready for school," can be all a child needs to stay on task. They will also take less of your energy.

CREATE A CONSISTENT SET OF REWARDS THAT YOUR CHILD CAN EARN BY GOOD BEHAVIOR

- Start small. Pick one or two behaviors to start with; for example, decreasing temper outbursts or talking back.
- Keep expectations simple. For example, when asked to clean his or her room or take his or her plate to the sink, the expectation is that your child will not argue, cry, shout, or produce some other undesirable response.
- Motivate your child by making a chart of his or her behavior.
- Use stickers or stars (tokens) to represent successful behavior. For example, if your child takes his or her plate to the sink without difficulty, he or she earns a star that is placed on the chart.
- Your child receives a reward, such as a small toy, a trip to the movies, or special time with a parent, after he or she earns a certain number of stars or tokens.
- Make earning stars within your child's reach. Behavior management through systems of reward work only when the child is able to see the consequences of good behavior. Set expectations that you know your child can meet, even if they fall short of the ideal behavior you'd like to see.
- Younger children need more immediate rewards. A week may be too long to associate good behavior with a reward. Try finding a reward that can be earned by a fewer number of stars or in one day, such as extra TV time or extra time on the computer.

- Your child's behavior may get worse before it gets better, as she or he "tests" how consistent the rules and consequences are.

PROVIDING STRUCTURE IS CRITICAL

- Establishing consistent rules and schedules goes a long way in helping your child manage tasks and activities.

DO NOT EXPECT MORE THAN YOUR CHILD CAN MANAGE

- Avoid too much stimulation. Many people with ADHD have trouble screening out the many sights and sounds that most people can ignore. Noisy places or the colorful multi-item displays used in stores may be overstimulating for your child and may make it difficult to control his or her behavior.
- Choose child care that has a low child-to-adult ratio.
- Avoid formal gatherings, shopping trips, or eating out if these are more than your child can handle.

PLAN AHEAD FOR DIFFICULT ENVIRONMENTS

- Set up a special reward or privilege for obeying established rules and behaving properly during an outing or event.
- Review rules and punishment (loss of privileges) prior to the event or outing.

PREPARE FOR TRANSITIONS

- Review the day's events in advance to help give your child an idea of what's going to happen.
- Give warnings fifteen, ten, and five minutes prior to a shift in activities or departure.

ROUTINE, ROUTINE, ROUTINE

- Meals, toileting, chores, and bedtime should be as regular as you can make them.

CATCH 'EM BEING GOOD

- Positive comments should outnumber negative comments by at least two to one; work toward a ratio of five to one.
- Tell your child what you like to see and comment when he or she does it. For example, "I liked the way you waited your turn to use the bike. You did a super job!"
- Ignore harmless negative behavior (annoying noises, repeated questions, etc.).

LET YOUR CHILD KNOW WHAT YOU WANT HIM OR HER TO DO

- Say "Walk, please" instead of "Don't run."
- Give only one instruction at a time.
- Some children with ADHD have a hard time listening when they are trying to do something else (i.e., tying shoes). Give your child important information when he or she can listen.
- Have a formal program of positive reinforcement in place at both home and school. Use tokens, stickers.

ESTABLISH CONSISTENT DISCIPLINE

- Less is more. Make a few clear rules and consistently enforce them.
- Act quickly. Talk (and threaten) less.
- Use nonphysical punishments: brief time-outs (young children) or loss of privileges (older children).

STRETCH HIS OR HER ATTENTION SPAN
- Reward nonhyperactive behavior with praise, a thumbs-up, or a hug.
- Limit play materials available at one time, but change them often.

COMMUNICATE FREQUENTLY WITH YOUR CHILD'S TEACHER
- Work together to make rules and consequences consistent.
- Speak up for your child.
- Educate teachers, family, and friends about ADHD.

GIVE CHILDREN FREQUENT, POSITIVE FEEDBACK
- Break activities into small steps.
- Create lists of steps to guide longer tasks.

PROVIDE A SAFE PLACE FOR FREE PLAY

Appendix B

SCHOOL SYSTEM INFORMATION AND RESOURCES

Your Child's Rights

It is important for parents to realize that there is a broad spectrum of services available to their children, all of which are protected under the Individuals with Disabilities Education Act (IDEA). Additionally, Section 504 of the Rehabilitation Act of 1973 forbids organizations, including schools, from excluding individuals with disabilities or denying them an equal opportunity to receive program benefits and services.

Individuals with Disabilities Act (IDEA)

The federal IDEA law requires that school districts provide special education services to students in a general education setting. General education settings are also called the least-restrictive environment (LRE) for students requiring special education services. Refer to chapter 11 for some of the special education services parents can request when their child's evaluations document deficiencies in various areas. All of these difficulties must be detailed on an Individual Education Plan (IEP).

As the needs of students become more pronounced, services in a general education setting may not be enough to foster their improvement in behavior, attention, or learning areas. It may also be necessary to consider special education programs if they are nearing a transition to middle or high school and you wish to get them as much help as possible before that transition. You may also consider placing a child in a special education program because all of the services delivered at different times by different providers are confusing or distracting.

Section 504

Many parents may encounter situations where their child is not eligible under IDEA for special services at school. If evaluation results indicate that your child is not eligible for services under IDEA, children with ADHD and/or other disabilities may qualify for an accommodation plan through Section 504 of the Rehabilitation Act. Section 504 specifically states that a local educational agency must offer a free suitable education in the least-restrictive environment for children with handicaps, provided the impairment is documented and continuous. Children who fit into this category are those who have a physical or mental condition, including ADHD, that significantly limits at least one major life activity (such as learning).

In order to provide a suitable education for the child, an accommodation plan can be developed for adjustments in a regular classroom. Additionally, remember to request that the accommodations decided upon be put in writing and signed by all parties involved (school and parents).

Section 504 is a civil rights law, so you can contact either the local school district or the civil rights office to ask questions to determine if this law is applicable to your child. Since each school district handles 504 plans differently, go first to your child's teacher and/or school administrators to find out how to contact the district 504 coordinators.

Put your request for a 504 plan in writing. Date and sign a letter that explains the purpose of the request by indicating where the concerns and problem areas lie. Some schools have forms for these "request for referral" letters. You will want to make a copy of this letter and, if possible, personally give the original to your child's school for its records. Upon delivery, the school is required to begin an evaluation process following strict and clearly defined guidelines.

If your child is deemed eligible under Section 504, the school district must develop a Section 504 plan. Unlike the IEP process, regulations for Section 504 do not specify the frequency of review of the plan or the role of outside evaluations, nor do they require parental involvement. However, you should be involved with every step of the process.

IDEA Versus Section 504

After a child is deemed eligible for services under IDEA and it has been determined that a child has special education needs, an IEP is created. Although an IEP and a 504 plan both provide services for children with ADHD, there are some differences between the two choices that you should be aware of.

- Eligibility for IDEA and an IEP requires that a child have a disability needing special education services, while eligibility for Section 504 may occur when the child needs special education *or* any related services.
- Children who have less severe disabilities and need minimal accommodations, who are otherwise not eligible for IDEA, may be covered under Section 504.
- There are far fewer rules and regulations placed on the testing process in Section 504 than are outlined with IDEA for an IEP. For example, Section 504 does not discuss the role of outside evaluations, limit the frequency of testing, or require parental consent for testing. Know your rights and what these programs can do for your child.
- The Section 504 process does require that an evaluation be conducted before a child receives a 504 plan and before any alterations are made to the proposed plan. In addition, because of the less strict safeguards provided by 504, parents should be aware that certain situations may arise that the 504 plan would not cover. These may include a "stay-put" provision to keep the child in his or her current environment while any issues are being resolved or having the plan travel with the child through the grades.

Resources

ADHD-Related Parent/Advocacy Organizations You Need to Know About

Anxiety Disorders Association of America
8730 Georgia Avenue, Suite 600
Silver Spring, MD 20910
(240) 485-1001 (tel)
(240) 485-1035 (fax)
information@adaa.org
www.adaa.org

Attention Deficit Disorder Association (ADDA)
15000 Commerce Parkway, Suite C
Mount Laurel, NJ 08054
(856) 439-9099 (tel)
(856) 439-0525 (fax)
www.add.org

Child and Adolescent Bipolar Foundation
1000 Skokie Boulevard, Suite 570
Wilmette, IL 60091
(847) 256-8525 (tel)
(847) 920-9498 (fax)
www.bpkids.org

Children and Adults with Attention Deficit Disorder (CHADD)
8181 Professional Place, Suite 150
Landover, MD 20785
(301) 306-7070 or (800) 233-4050 (tel)
(301) 306-7090 (fax)
www.chadd.org

Depression and Bipolar Support Alliance
730 N. Franklin Street, Suite 501
Chicago, Illinois 60610-7224
(800) 826-3632 (tel)
(312) 642-7243 (fax)
www.dbsalliance.org

Learning Disabilities Association of America (LDA)
4156 Library Road
Pittsburgh, PA 15234-1349
(412) 341-1515 (tel)
(412) 344-0224 (fax)
www.ldanatl.org

Mental Health America
2000 N. Beauregard Street, 6th floor
Alexandria, VA 22311
(703) 684-7722 (tel)
(703) 684-5968 (fax)
www.nmha.org

National Alliance on Mental Illness (NAMI)
Colonial Place Three
2107 Wilson Boulevard, Suite 300
Arlington, VA 22201-3042
(703) 524-7600 (tel)
(800) 950-6264 (NAMI helpline)
www.nami.org

National Federation of Families for Children's Mental Health (FFCMH)
9605 Medical Center Drive, Suite 280
Rockville, MD 20850
(240) 403-1901 (tel)
(240) 403-1909 (fax)
www.ffcmh.org

Parents Helping Parents: Parent-Directed Family Resource Center for Children with Special Needs
3041 Olcott Street
Santa Clara, CA 95054
(408) 727-5775 (tel)
(408) 727-0182 (fax)
info@php.com
www.php.com

Related websites Useful for Parents

American Academy of Child and Adolescent Psychiatry
3615 Wisconsin Avenue, N.W.
Washington, DC 20016-3007

(202) 966-7300 (tel)
(202) 966-2891 (fax)
www.aacap.org

> The American Academy of Child and Adolescent
> Psychiatry is the nation's leading professional
> organization for child and adolescent psychiatrists.
> This organization provides much useful information
> on child psychiatric providers, as well as Facts for
> Families, tip sheets that can be downloaded on a
> variety of subjects of interest to parents and families
> concerning child mental health.

American Academy of Pediatrics
141 Northwest Point Boulevard
Elk Grove Village, IL 60007-1098
(847) 434-4000
www.aap.org

> The American Academy of Pediatrics is the nation's
> leading organization for pediatricians. This
> organization provides much useful information on
> pediatric health, including ADHD, child development,
> and other topics of interest to parents and families
> concerning child mental health.

National Resource Center on AD/HD
8181 Professional Place, Suite 100
Landover, MD 20785
(800) 233-4050
www.help4adhd.org

> The National Resource Center on AD/HD is a program
> of CHADD that was established with funding from

the U.S. Centers for Disease Control and Prevention to be a national clearinghouse of information and resources concerning ADHD, an important public health concern. This website is chock-full of all types of information useful to parents and families of a child with ADHD.

The REACH Institute (Resource for Advancing Children's Health)

450 Seventh Avenue, Suite 1107
New York, NY 10123
(212) 947-7322 (tel)
(212) 947-7400 (fax)
www.thereachinstitute.org

The REACH Institute is the premier nonprofit national organization committed to ensuring that parents and families have local access to health care providers trained in using the latest diagnostic and treatment methods to aid children with ADHD and other behavioral health problems across the United States.

Technical Assistance Alliance for Parent Centers

8161 Normandale Boulevard
Minneapolis, MN 55437-1044
(952) 838-9000 or (888) 248-0822 (tel)
(952) 838-0199 (fax)
alliance@taalliance.org
www.taalliance.org

Learning to advocate for your child is a critical step that all parents of children with ADHD need to undertake so that they can secure services for their

children and ensure the success of their children in
all facets of life. Funded by the U.S. Department of
Education, Office of Special Education Programs,
the Technical Assistance Alliance for Parent Centers
establishes and coordinates parent training centers
nationwide. These training centers, Parent Training and
Information Centers and Community Parent Resource
Centers, serve families of children and young adults
(from birth to age twenty-two) with disabilities. There
are approximately one hundred parent centers in the
United States.

Funding and Insurance-Related Resources You Need to Know About

Directory of State Insurance Departments
www.naic.org
> Each state has its own insurance department to oversee
> all types of insurance. This website provides links to
> each state office.

Insurance Information
www.ahip.org
> Under "Quick Links," choose "Health Insurance Plan
> Site Links" for a directory of health insurance plans.

Medicaid
www.cms.hhs.gov/home/Medicaid.asp?
> Medicaid is a jointly funded, federal-state health
> insurance program for certain low-income and

needy people. Within broad national guidelines
that the federal government provides, each of the
states establishes its own eligibility standards;
determines the type, amount, duration, and scope of
services; sets the rate of payment for services; and
administers its own program. Thus, the Medicaid
program varies considerably from state to state, as
well as within each state over time. The Centers for
Medicare and Medicaid Services (CMS) offer a wealth
of information and a directory of state Medicaid
offices on their website. It lists various resources and
technical guidance such as state medicaid manuals,
fraud and abuse information, and Medicaid statistics
and data.

National Resource Center on AD/HD
www.help4adhd.org/en/systems/public
The National Resource Center on AD/HD: A Program
of CHADD has been established with funding from
the U.S. Centers for Disease Control and Prevention
(CDC) to be a national clearinghouse of information
and resources concerning ADHD, an important public
health concern. People with mental disorders may be
eligible for several forms of public assistance to meet
the basic costs of living and to pay for health care. This
website lists information on Supplemental Security
Income (SSI), Social Security Disability Insurance
(SSDI), and Temporary Assistance to Needy Families
(TANF).

Pharmaceutical Research and Manufacturers of America (PhRMA)

www.helpingpatients.org

PhRMA is the trade association for pharmaceutical and biotechnology companies. PhRMA's mission is winning advocacy for public policies that encourage the discovery of lifesaving and life-enhancing new medications for patients by pharmaceutical/ biotechnology research companies. The Helping Patients website offers an online directory of patient assistance programs run by more than forty of its member companies.

U.S. Department of Health and Human Services, State Children's Health Insurance Program

www.cms.hhs.gov/home/schip.asp

The U.S. Department of Health and Human Services oversees the State Children's Health Insurance Program (S-CHIP), which provides the nation's ten million uninsured children with free or low-cost health insurance. Every state has a health insurance program for infants, children, and teens whose families do not qualify for Medicaid. Many families simply don't know that their children are eligible. The states have different eligibility rules, but in most states, uninsured children eighteen years old and younger whose families earn up to $34,100 a year (for a family of four) are eligible. This website lists information for each state about health insurance for infants, children, and adolescents. The toll-free number is (877) KIDS-NOW.

Legal/Advocacy Resources You Need to Know About

Judge David L. Bazelon Center for Mental Health Law
www.bazelon.org

The Bazelon Center is an information and advocacy organization that focuses on laws, policies, and regulations that affect the civil rights of people with mental disabilities and access to services for adults and children with disabilities.

NAMI Legal Publications: Legal Protection and Advocacy for People with Severe Mental Illnesses in Managed Care Systems
www.nami.org/Content/ContentGroups/Legal/NAMI_ Legal_Publications.htm

This NAMI resource provides an overview of legal issues in both the public and private sectors. The manual is a blueprint for challenging decisions and practices in often-complicated systems.

Your State Protection and Advocacy System
www.napas.org/aboutus/PA_CAP.htm

To obtain legal representation, please contact the protection and advocacy system in your state. Protection and advocacy (P&A) systems in each state are federally funded to assist people with mental or developmental disabilities in understanding and asserting their rights. Other aids include the free online resource from the Commission on Mental and Physical Disability Law at www.abanet.org/disability. You may also find other agencies in your state on the Bazelon

Center website's list of state advocacy links at www.
bazelon.org/links/states/index.htm.

Useful Books

Books on ADHD for Parents

Making the System Work for Your Child with ADHD
Peter S. Jensen
Guilford Press, 2004, 300 pages

In this empowering, highly informative book, parents
learn the whats, whys, and how-tos of making the
system work—getting their money's worth from
the health-care system, cutting through red tape at
school, and making the most of fleeting time with
doctors and therapists. Dr. Jensen interweaves the
combined wisdom of more than eighty parents with
his own insights as an expert practitioner and the
father of a child with ADHD. Packed with planning
tips, resources, moral support, and problem-solving
strategies that get results, this is a book that savvy
parents will turn to again and again.

*Taking Charge of ADHD: The Complete Authoritative
Guide for Parents*
Russell A. Barkley
Guilford Press, 1995, 294 pages

This is an outstanding resource for parents of children
with attention deficit disorder with hyperactivity.
Taking Charge of ADHD has now been revised and
updated to incorporate the most current information

on ADHD and its treatment. From internationally renowned ADHD expert Russell A. Barkley, the book empowers parents by arming them with the up-to-date knowledge, expert guidance, and confidence they need to ensure that their child receives the best care possible.

Books on ADHD for Kids and Teens

A Bird's-Eye View of Life with ADD and ADHD: Advice from Young Survivors
Chris A. Zeigler Dendy and Alex Zeigler
Cherish the Children, 2003, 180 pages
> This book is a treasured resource for teenagers that gives firsthand advice from their peers. It was written by twelve teens and a young adult who are living with ADHD. In addition to factual information and practical strategies, this book gives teens and families a sense of hope that they too will survive this sometimes overwhelming disorder.

Learning to Slow Down and Pay Attention: A Book for Kids About ADD
Kathleen G. Nadeau and Ellen B. Dixon; illustrations by John Rose
Magination Press, 1997, 80 pages
> This workbook gives kids with ADD information on such matters as how to clean a room quickly and easily and how to make sure they do their homework on time. It is a fun-filled approach to learning how to get along better at school, with friends, and in life. The

book is packed with cartoons, games, and activities. For parents, the book includes information on behavior management and on support groups.

Books on ADHD for Teachers

Teaching Teens with ADD and ADHD: A Quick Reference Guide for Teachers and Parents
Chris A. Zeigler Dendy
Woodbine House, 2000, 352 pages

This book contains everything a teacher needs to know about attention deficit disorder in teens. *Teaching Teens with ADD and ADHD* contains concise summaries of more than fifty key issues related to attention deficit disorder and school success. Topics range from understanding the basics of ADD to using effective interventions.

Books on ADHD for All

ADHD Handbook for Families: A Guide to Communicating with Professionals
Paul L. Weingartner
Child Welfare League of America, 1999, 146 pages

This book is packed with proven, real-life strategies and techniques that can be put to use immediately. It is an excellent resource for anyone who wants to understand what ADHD is, what it feels like, and how to help children live a full life.

Attention Deficit Hyperactivity Disorder: State of the Science, Best Practices
Peter Jensen and James Cooper, editors
Civic Research Institute, 2002

Written by researchers in the field of children's mental health, this book details the current best practices for ADHD. It is an in-depth guide to ADHD diagnosis, causes, treatment, and outcomes. Topics include biological bases and cognitive correlates of ADHD; controversies regarding over- and underdiagnosis of ADHD; risks and rewards of treatment with stimulant medication; the impact on individuals, families, and society; and much more. This book encompasses an overall view of the state of the science of ADHD.

Driven to Distraction: Recognizing and Coping with Attention Deficit Disorder from Childhood Through Adulthood
Edward M. Hallowell and John J. Ratey
Touchstone Books, 1995, 336 pages

This clear and valuable book dispels a variety of myths about attention deficit disorder. The authors attack the two most specific myths: (1) that ADD is an issue only for children, and (2) that ADD relates simply to limited intelligence or limited self-discipline. The authors blatantly attack these myths with their own personal lives: both authors have ADD themselves and both are successful medical professionals. They cite Mozart and Einstein as examples of possible ADD sufferers. Although they warn against overdiagnosis, they also do a convincing job of answering the criticism that "everybody and therefore nobody" has ADD. Especially helpful are the lists of tips for dealing with ADD in a child, a partner, or a family member.

Books on Medication

Pocket Guide for the Textbook of Pharmacotherapy for Child and Adolescent Psychiatric Disorders
David Rosenberg, John Holttum, Neal Ryan, and Samuel Gershon
Brunner/Mazel, 1994, 555 pages
> This is a quick reference guide for psychiatrists, therapists, social workers, and other practitioners about each group of medications. It is a comprehensive textbook that focuses on diagnostic issues relevant to dispensing psychotropic medications to children and adolescents, highlighting similarities and differences in treating children versus adults.

Helping Parents, Youth, and Teachers Understand Medications for Behavioral and Emotional Problems: A Resource Book of Medication Information Handouts
Mina K. Dulcan and Tami Benton, editors
American Psychiatric Press, 2002, 202 pages
> This book was developed by experts at Children's Memorial Hospital in Chicago. It is a collection of handouts that cover today's most effective medications for pediatric behavioral and emotional disorders, including anticonvulsants, stimulants, antianxiety medications, and SSRIs.

Straight Talk About Psychiatric Medications for Kids
(revised edition)
Timothy E. Wilens
Guilford Press, 2004

> This essential book provides the up-to-date information
> that will enable readers to fully understand what their
> child's doctor is recommending, and what their options
> are. Harvard University researcher and practitioner
> Dr. Timothy Wilens explains which medications may be
> prescribed for children, and why; examines effects on
> children's health, emotions, and school performance;
> and helps parents become active, informed managers of
> their children's care.

Books on Behavioral Therapy

*ADD and the College Student: A Guide for High School
and College Students with Attention Deficit Disorder*
Patricia O. Quinn, editor
Magination Press, 1994, 128 pages

> This concise handbook is packed with practical
> information and advice for the smoothest possible
> transition to college life, including lifestyle habits for a
> student's success.

*The ADHD Book of Lists: A Practical Guide for Helping
Children and Teens with Attention Deficit Disorders*
Sandra F. Rief
Jossey-Bass, 2003, 320 pages

> This book is a comprehensive, reliable source of answers,
> practical strategies, and tools written in a convenient

list format. It is filled with the strategies, supports, and interventions that have been found to be the most effective in minimizing the problems and optimizing the success of children and teens with ADHD.

The Organized Parent: 365 Simple Solutions to Managing Your Home, Your Time, and Your Family's Life
Christina Tinglof
McGraw Hill, 2002, 256 pages
This book contains a collection of tips and advice on how you can create an organized and efficient home and family schedule.

Think Good—Feel Good: A Cognitive Behavior Therapy Workbook for Children
Paul Stallard
Halsted Press, 2002, 186 pages
This book is an exciting and pioneering new practical resource for undertaking cognitive-behavioral therapy with children and young people. The materials have been developed by the author and tested extensively in clinical work with children and young people presenting with a range of psychological problems.

Treating Anger, Anxiety, and Depression in Children and Adolescents: A Cognitive-Behavioral Perspective
Jerry Wilde
Accelerated Development, 1996, 185 pages
This is a guide to treating the most prevalent problems facing children and adolescents today, using rational-

emotive behavior therapy. The author applies a cognitive-behavioral perspective in individual, group, school, or private settings.

You Mean I'm Not Lazy, Stupid or Crazy?!: A Self-help Book for Adults with Attention Deficit Disorder
Kate Kelly, Peggy Ramundo, and Larry B. Silver
Scribner, 1996, 464 pages
This book contains straightforward, practical advice for taking control of the symptoms, minimizing the disabilities, and maximizing the advantages of adult ADD.

Organization and Time Management

Organization and time management present challenges for many people but can be especially challenging for individuals with ADHD. The hallmark traits of ADHD, inattention and distractibility, make organization and management of time and money very difficult, requiring the individual to implement various structures and processes and to utilize tools such as day planners and reminders.

Other helpful tips for organization skills:

- Use to-do lists and day planners
- Use timers and alarms, either through a clock, watch, PDA, or computer
- Attend to daily tasks, such as filing documents or paying bills
- Color-code file folders, textbooks, and binders

- Designate specific areas for easily misplaced items such as keys and bills
- Break down large projects into smaller, manageable steps

BOOKS AND WEBSITES ON ORGANIZATION/HOME AND TIME MANAGEMENT

Hall, Janet. "OverHall" Your Life and Spaces: Solutions for Healthier Bodies and Environments; www.overhall .com.

Kolberg, J., and K. Nadeau. *ADD-Friendly Ways to Organize Your Life*. New York: Brunner-Routledge, 2002.

Morgenstern, J. *Organizing from the Inside Out*. New York: Henry Holt, 1998.

Schechter, H. *Let Go of Clutter*. New York: McGraw-Hill, 2001; www.letgoclutter.com.

Winston, S. *Stephanie Winston's Best Organizing Tips*. New York: Simon and Schuster, 1995.

Index

About the Authors

EDWARD M. HALLOWELL, M.D., was an instructor at Harvard Medical School for twenty years and is now the director of the Hallowell Centers for Cognitive and Emotional Health in Sudbury, Massachusetts, and New York City. He is the co-author of *Delivered from Distraction* and *Driven to Distraction* as well as the author of *CrazyBusy, The Childhood Roots of Adult Happiness,* and *Worry,* among other titles. He lives in Arlington, Massachusetts, with his wife and their three children.

www.DrHallowell.com

PETER S. JENSEN, M.D., is a world-renowned child psychiatrist, the author of more than 200 scientific articles, and the CEO of the REACH (REsource for Advancing Children's Health) Institute. Dr. Jensen was the founding director of the Center for the Advancement of Children's Mental Health at Columbia University and the associate director of Child and Adolescent Research at NIMH, where he served from 1989 to 2000. In 1999 he received the Exemplary Psychiatrist Award from NAMI (the National Alliance for the Mentally Ill) and was inducted into the Hall of Fame for Children and Adults with Attention-Deficit/ Hyperactivity Disorder. He lives in New York.